Identity Formation in the Adopted Adolescent

THE DELAWARE FAMILY STUDY

LESLIE M. STEIN
JANET L. HOOPES

The Delaware Family Study
Child Welfare League of America, Inc.

Child Welfare League of America
67 Irving Place, New York, NY 10003

Current printing (last digit)
10 9 8 7 6 5 4 3 2 1

Printed in the United States of America

Cover and text design by Meri Duskin

Library of Congress Cataloging in Publication Data

Stein, Leslie M.
    Identity formation in the adopted adolescent.

    "The Delaware Family Study."
    Bibliography: p.
    1. Adoptees — Psychology. 2. Identity (Psychology)
3. Youth — Psychology.   I. Hoopes, Janet L.   II. Title
HV875.S693   1985   155.5   84-29373
ISBN 0-87868-234-1

The Authors

Leslie M. Stein is Assistant Professor in the Department of Child Care at Temple University. She received her doctorate from Bryn Mawr College and is currently a licensed clinical psychologist and certified school psychologist in Pennsylvania. In the past, Dr. Stein has served as Director of Children's Services in a mental health center in Delaware County, Pennsylvania. In addition to her teaching responsibilities, Dr. Stein has a private practice.

Janet L. Hoopes is Professor of Human Development and Director of the Child Study Institute at Bryn Mawr College, from which she received her doctoral degree. She is a certified school psychologist and licensed clinical psychologist in Pennsylvania and served for 20 years as psychologist with the Children's Aid Society of Pennsylvania. Dr. Hoopes is the author or co-author of four research studies, including *An Infant Rating Scale: Its Validation and Usefulness*, and three studies of adoption, all published by the Child Welfare League of America.

ACKNOWLEDGMENTS

THIS STUDY WAS FUNDED by a grant from the Children's Bureau of Wilmington, Delaware. The grant supported the Delaware Family Study, a longitudinal research project on adoptive families begun in 1962.*

A research project of this size could not have been executed without the contributions and support of many persons, to whom we are deeply indebted.

First and foremost, special thanks and appreciation to the families and teenagers of the Delaware Family Study, whose unflagging interest and cooperation made this whole project possible.

To the entire staff of the Children's Bureau of Wilmington, Delaware, our thanks for their gracious accommodation and helpfulness in the interviewing stage of this project. Special acknowledgment goes to Barbara Stager, Chairperson of the Research Committee of the Board of the Children's Bureau, Demo N. Carros, Executive Director of the Children's Bureau, and Susan Burns, whose coordinative efforts in the project were greatly appreciated.

We are particularly grateful to Elizabeth von Frankenberg, whose talent and sensitivity as liaison between the families and this final phase of research contributed to the overall success of the project.

Many thanks to the students of the Haverford and Radnor Township School Districts, whose participation in the project was invaluable to its com-

---

* For the first volume of data from this project, see Janet L. Hoopes, *Prediction in Child Development: A Longitudinal Study of Adoptive and Nonadoptive Families* (New York, NY: The Child Welfare League of America, 1982).

pletion. Special appreciation to Dr. David Heckman and Deborah Batchelor of the Haverford School District and Lois Adams and Robert Fitzgerald of the Radnor School District for their willingness to sponsor a project of this nature. Our gratitude to the guidance departments of both school districts for their investment of time in the scheduling of interviews.

Special thanks to Cliff Nesbit and Dr. Thomas Treadwell for their valuable consultation on the Social Atom.

To Dr. Jerry Kominsarof and Penny Glackman, the deepest gratitude for their tireless editing and moral support.

Thanks also go to Mary Lovell, whose professionalism, patience, and precision in the typing of this manuscript seemed to have no bounds.

CONTENTS

TABLES

CHAPTER *1*

*E*GO IDENTITY:
SOME THEORETICAL QUESTIONS

*F*OR SEVERAL DECADES now, the study of adoption has generated intense debate on the level of both theory and practice alike. In addition, adoption research has produced a plethora of contradictory findings, leaving the practitioner in a quandary as to their applicability. Although Hoopes (Hoopes et al. 1970; 1982) reports that the overwhelming majority of adoptions can be considered successful, the bulk of the literature on comparative findings between adopted and nonadopted children suggests that adopted individuals are susceptible to greater social and emotional stress (Goodman et al. 1963; Schecter et al. 1964; Simon and Senturia 1966; Toussieng 1962). These studies do deserve some mention, but it is important to note that the preponderance of comparative research has been based on psychiatric case studies and clinic populations. Some authors (Hoopes et al. 1970; Witmer et al. 1963) have refuted these findings on the basis that the self-selection of clinical populations permits no comparisons with the general population. Unfortunately, as Kirk and associates (1966) have aptly stated, criticisms of this nature rarely come to the attention of the informed reading public.

Clearly, there has been a paucity of controlled, systematic research using normative populations of adopted and nonadopted youngsters. The Delaware Family Study, a longitudinal study of adopted and biological children begun in 1962 (Hoopes 1982), is one of a few comparative efforts that have attempted to fill the void in normative adoption research. Although this and other works (Bohman 1972; Witmer et al. 1963) have examined the development and adjustment of adopted children vis-a-vis their nonadopted counterparts, very little research to date has focused specifically on the adopted individual's adjustment in adolescence. The current study is an attempt to broaden our knowledge about the impact of adoption on the adolescent years, with the hope of unraveling some of the complexities that adoption brings to the experience of adolescence.

OBJECTIVES OF THE STUDY

Most authors on adoption and adolescence report that the adopted adolescent does in fact have greater difficulty with the tasks of this stage (Frisk 1964; Tec and Gordon 1967; Sorosky et al. 1975). The main purpose of the present study is to test empirically major theoretical assumptions about the identity challenges that adoption poses. This is accomplished through a comparison of 15- to 18-year-old adolescent adoptees and nonadoptees drawn from a nonclinical population. This study is largely an exploratory one that additionally seeks to determine what factors enhance or impede the resolution of identity issues in the adopted adolescent with the intent of isolating those factors that contribute positively to the process.

Specifically, this research addresses the following questions: How does being adopted impinge on the process of identity formation during adolescence? Does being adopted adversely affect an adolescent's consolidation of ego identity, as some of the literature suggests? If significant differences in identity formation and adjustment exist between the two groups of adolescents, are the problems related to the fact of adoption or to other variables that might be compounding the process of identity formation in some adolescents? Finally, what differentiates those adopted adolescents who express an avid wish to search for their biological parents from those who show no such wish? The last question is of particular interest in light of the present debate over the unsealing of adoption records.

The study has two major functions. The first is to add to the area of normative research on both adoption and adolescence by offering an empirical investigation of adolescence proper and the adolescence of adoptees in particular. The present study is unique in that it uses a nonclinical population of adoptees within an age group that has not heretofore been investigated. Likewise, few studies have ever sought to ask adopted adolescents directly for a phenomenological account of what it is like to be adopted. The second function of this study is to provide a bridge between psychological theory, empirical observation, and practical application. More specifically, it is hoped that this research will provide useful guidelines for adoptive families and practitioners who work with adopted adolescents.

THE CONCEPT OF EGO IDENTITY

A study of the effects of adoption on the consolidation of ego identity in adolescence must begin with a discussion of the main developmental task of this period. The period of adolescence has been identified by many writers as a time marked by the primary task of identity formation (Blos 1970; Douvan and Adelson 1966; Erikson 1950; Marcia 1967). During these years, the adolescent's major goal is generally thought to be the construction and crystallization of a well-delineated identity. Spiegel (1959) has asserted that one of the purposes of adolescence within the total developmental line of the individual is the achievement of a firm sense of self. Exactly what is meant by "identity" or "sense of self" is not so easy to interpret, although different theoretical perspectives have sought to provide a clearer definition of these rather vague concepts.

Despite the elusive and complex constructs of contemporary psychoanalytic theory, it has been most instrumental both in stimulating identity research and in providing a comprehensive theoretical framework for understanding some of the actual phenomena observed in the clinical study of personality formation. For these reasons, it is the perspective selected for a theoretical and empirical investigation of "ego identity."

The Writings of Erik Erikson

Erik Erikson (1950, 1959, 1963) has perhaps been the most influential ego-psychoanalytic theoretician on identity. He views identity as an epigenetically based psychosocial task distinctive to adolescence. According to Erikson (1959), the term "identity" is multidimensional, referring to

a conscious sense of individual identity at one time; at
another, to an unconscious striving for a continuity of personal character; at a third, as a criterion for the silent doings
of ego synthesis; and finally, as a maintenance of an inner
solidarity with a group's ideals and identity. (p. 102)

For Erikson (1959, 118), a conscious sense of identity refers to the achievement of an inner cohesiveness and self-definition whose by-product is a feeling of psychosocial well-being reflecting "an inner assuredness of anticipated recognition from those who count."

When Erikson speaks of "an unconscious striving for a continuity of personal character," he is simultaneously referring to the establishment of a feeling of connectedness between one's past, present, and future as well as the achievement of unity among the various ascribed and achieved social roles and skills that the adolescent must integrate in the course of time (Bourne 1978). In adolescence, "all samenesses and continuities relied on earlier are more or less questioned again, because of the rapidity of body growth and because of the new addition of genital maturity" (Erikson 1950, 261).

In his conception of identity as an integrative phenomenon, Erikson (1959) sees identity formation as an ongoing process that has its roots in the earliest stages of growth. According to his epigenetic principle of personality growth, the foundations of identity are laid down in the successful resolution of earlier psychosocial "crises" of childhood, that is, "basic trust vs. mistrust," "autonomy vs. shame or doubt," "initiative vs. guilt" and "industry vs. inferiority," that contribute to an accruing sense of ego strength in the adolescent.

Briefly, a lasting ego identity cannot begin to exist without (1) the mutual trustworthiness of the first stage of development, (2) the sense of autonomy, independence, self-control, and pride stemming from the second stage, (3) the curiosity, ambition, and ability to experiment with different roles resulting from the third stage, and (4) the desire for mastery, accomplishment, and recognition from others that follows from a successful involvement with the tasks of industry at the fourth stage (Erikson 1959). In the end, a successful traversal of all four stages results in the achievement of a healthy sense of self-esteem. Erikson (1959, 116) maintains that identity is a developmental end product "gradually integrating constitutional givens, idiosyncratic libidinal needs, favored capacities, significant identifications, affective defenses, successful sublimations and consistent roles." As a structural component of the personality, it is thus easy to see how Marcia (1980) has concluded that the more consolidated the identity, the better the individual's adaptation will be to the demands of the prevailing role structure of the society in which he or she lives.

The integration taking place in the form of an evolving identity is more than the sum of childhood identifications, however. Rather, it is a new entity arising from the selective repudiation and mutual assimilation of the adolescent's identification with his or her parents, as well as with others outside the family. In this fashion, "identity formation begins where the usefulness of identification ends" (Erikson 1959, 113). While Erikson points to the uniqueness and independence that accompany the newfound sense of identity, he nevertheless stresses the importance of a solid anchoring within the family, in which the adolescent's history of positive identification with the parent of the same sex and a stable, growth-productive relationship with the parent of the opposite sex together contribute to the establishment of a solid sense of sexual identity in adolescence.

Finally, Erikson (1959) attributes a sense of psychosocial mutuality to identity, implying a reciprocal relationship with one's immediate community or peer group. In the development of a social self-definition, the adolescent attempts a meaningful consolidation of social roles through peer interaction and the commitment to a peer group. The adolescent is eager to be affirmed by his or her peers in a persistent sharing of some kind of essential character with them. It is this "psychosocial" aspect that distinguishes ego identity from other conceptions of self (Bourne 1978).

Margaret Mahler and Peter Blos:
A Psychoanalytic Expansion of the Identity Concept

Two writers who have focused on the long-term intrapsychic developmental processes essential to identity formation are Margaret Mahler (1968) and Peter Blos (1967). According to Mahler and colleagues (1975), a sense of individual identity is the developmental outcome of the separation-individuation process, which consists of two complementary developments: (1) separation, that is, the child's emergence on an object-relational level from the symbiotic fusion with the mother; and (2) individuation, that is, the child's intrapsychic achievements that mark the assumption of his or her own individual characteristics. This latter process is brought about by the evolution and expansion of autonomous ego functions that center on the developing self-concept (Mahler 1968). Like Erikson, Mahler alludes to a sense of autonomy and self-esteem that normally evolves in the earliest stages of growth.

While Mahler addresses herself to the original infantile process mediating the achievement of a sense of separateness and identity, Blos (1970) focuses on the issue of identity consolidation in adolescence, citing the newly emerging maturational events of puberty that tend to reactivate old issues of separation and individuation. Blos (1967, 62) conceives of a sense of personal identity as emanating from the "shedding of family dependencies and loosening of infantile object ties" that allow for a "second individuation." In adolescence, this latter process involves a taking on of unique characteristics that result in a highly idiosyncratic and stable arrangement of ego functions and interests (Blos 1962).

According to Blos (1967), the adolescent's separation process occurs at two levels — object-relational and intrapsychic. Interpersonally, the adolescent is involved in the withdrawal of some emotional energy from the parents as significant objects and the reinvestment of this energy in peer relationships. This can be observed clinically in the adolescent's growing capacity for heterosexual object finding (Blos 1968). Intrapsychically, a disengagement from early childhood identifications with the parent must occur, allowing sufficient freedom to assimilate new models provided by a more diverse group of society's representatives, such as teachers, peers, heroes, and ideals. Without this disengagement, identity formation is stalemated. In summary, then, Blos (1962, 128) maintains that with the consolidation of identity, the adolescent "registers gains in purposeful action, social integration, predictability, constancy of emotions and stability of self-esteem."

James Marcia: The Identity Status Paradigm

James Marcia (1980), known for his theoretical and empirical expansions of Eriksonian theory, views identity as an evolving, dynamic entity involving numerous reorganizations of contents throughout one's life. He diverges from Erikson in (1) his emphasis on the existential quality of ego identity, that is, the meaning one attributes to life in the form of "basic life commitments"; and (2) his focus on the changeability of identity contents throughout a person's life. According to Marcia (1980, 160), "identity involves commitment to a sexual orientation, an ideological stance, and a vocational direction," in contrast to Erikson's definition, which is more elemental. Marcia asserts that the individual's commitments are what provide him or her with a definition of self.

Marcia proposes that the identity formation process consists of repeated negations and affirmations as the adolescent is exposed to life's many choices. More specifically, it is the "style" of decison making or choosing that forms the basis of the individual's identity structure and provides a means of characterizing identity types. By studying an adolescent's problem-solving responses to choice, Marcia maintains that one is actually able to glimpse the underlying organization called "identity."

Daniel Offer: An Empirical Approach to Identity

A more empirically based treatment of the concept of self is provided by Offer and his colleagues (Offer et al. 1981). They use the term as Douvan and Adelson (1966) did, to denote "the observed person's phenomenological experiences of the self." While Offer and colleagues acknowledge an unconscious component to the phenomenal self, they dismiss the saliency of those unconscious self-feelings, maintaining that what the normal adolescent consciously perceives about himself or herself and is willing to report is significantly more compelling and informative. They even go so far as to state that an adolescent unable to acknowledge conscious self-feelings could be evaluated as emotionally unhealthy.

A major goal of Offer's research on the adolescent self-image was to elucidate the nature of the self in general. Using a self-image questionnaire approach, Offer identified five separate aspects of the adolescent's self-system amenable to evaluation. These "selves," representing discrete areas of concern, are the psychological self, the social self, the family self, the sexual self, and the coping self. To the extent that the adolescent may feel differently about himself or herself in different contexts (e.g., as a student, friend, son or daughter), the adolescent can be thought of as having many selves or self-dimensions (Offer 1981).

For Offer (1981, 11), the adolescent's "desire to know the self is tied up with learning how to relate to others while also acquiring a sense of separateness and autonomy, the quest to achieve what Erikson calls identity." Thus, while Offer avoids direct reference to the term "identity" in his own writings, his theoretical overlap with Erikson, Blos, and Marcia is strikingly apparent.

TOWARD A MEASUREMENT OF EGO IDENTITY

Searching for the behavioral referents of individuation or identity presents a challenge to those interested in research along these lines. With the exception of the voluminous work of Marcia (1966), attempts at defining ego identity for research purposes have been sparse.

Marcia (1966) developed "identity statuses" as a methodological means of subjecting Erikson's concepts to empirical study. His empirical efforts have focused on the delineation and validation of four styles or modes of reacting to the Eriksonian identity crisis of late adolescence. These modes are defined in terms of (1) the presence or absence of a period of crisis, that is, a time in which the adolescent is actively involved in choosing among alternative behaviors and beliefs, and (2) the degree of commitment in the areas of occupation and ideology, specifically, religious and political beliefs (Marcia 1966). Marcia believes that the degree of ego identity achieved is based on the presence or absence of these two variables. For example, identity achievement subjects have experienced a period of crisis and decision making and have made firm occupational and ideological commitments; moratorium individuals are currently in a state of crisis, testing alternative commitments but making no decisions as yet; foreclosures have settled on an identity through the assimilation of parental values and beliefs without having experienced crisis; finally, identity diffusion individuals have shown little ability to commit themselves to an occupation or set of ideological beliefs regardless of the presence of crisis.

The identity status interview was designed by Marcia (1966) to enable the classification of individuals according to their style of identity resolution. Marcia's identity status approach poses several problems, however, that impede its implementation in the present study. First, nearly all the studies employing Marcia's paradigm have been confined to college populations (Bourne 1978b). The validity of basing the total identity status of high school students on a statement of occupational and ideological commitment is, in the authors' opinion, rather questionable. Not only might there be other more identity-salient areas of commitment for this age group, but the qualitative differences between high school and college groups might very well invalidate Marcia's interview for high school populations or at least significantly lower the discriminant validity of the statuses.

Furthermore, studies (Marcia 1976b; Waterman 1974, as reported in Bourne 1978a) investigating the long-term stability of the identity statuses have found that they are not particularly stable over long periods of time, that is, they do not readily predict identity status several years later. For this reason, even Marcia (1976b) recognizes the advantages of conceptualizing identity in terms of an ongoing process instead of the more categorical identity statuses.

Finally, and perhaps most importantly, the substantive issue arises about whether Marcia's more existential and empirically rigorous approach to identity captures the crux of what Erikson (1950; 1959; 1968) has theorized. Again, the authors believe that there is much more to identity than stated occupational and ideological commitments, particularly as regards a high school population. Marcia himself seemed to have some awareness of this.

> I am very much aware that what has been dealt with...are some surface manifestations of identity and that their referent is a much more highly concentrated group of processes ordinarily inaccessible to direct observation. (quoted in Bourne 1978b, 377)

Because of the methodological and substantive problems mentioned above, the identity status paradigm has been rejected as a viable methodology for the present study. After considering alternative methods of studying identity, the authors selected contemporary psychoanalytic concepts of adolescent development as a theoretical framework for investigating the process of identity formation.

Assessment Variables

Having considered some of the more influential, psychodynamic conceptualizations of ego identity, from the most theoretical to the more empirically based, it seems possible to cull from the various authors some of the components of the identity concept that might be most relevant to the current research. Although most of the theorists reviewed tend to speak of inferred intrapsychic states rather than behavioral conditions, several of the constructs seem to lend themselves to empirical examination and have, in fact, served as dependent variables in research on identity. These include autonomy and individuation, industry and mastery, initiative and sexuality, and self-image and self-esteem. As these variables are often viewed in terms of their behavioral correlates in the adolescent, the following contexts are used in this study to assess adolescent growth along the dimension of identity formation: (1) relatedness within one's family; (2) peer relations or social competence; (3) sexuality or sex-role identity; (4) school performance; and (5) self-image or self-esteem. A brief overview and rationale for each of these areas follows.

Family Relatedness

According to Erikson (1963), a sense of relatedness within one's family is essential in providing the adolescent with stable, reliable, and positively endowed objects for the purpose of identification, one of the forerunners of identity formation. The lack of positive models for identification leaves the adolescent vulnerable and susceptible to feelings of insecurity and worthlessness. Predicated on a sense of positive parental relationship is the growth of autonomy and individuation, both by-products of and preconditions for identity formation, as conceived by Erikson (1959) and Blos (1967).

Peer Relations/Social Competence

The area of peer relations is of crucial importance, according to Blos (1962), because it is during adolescence that the child more completely transfers his or her interests and emotional attachments from the family to the outside world. Acceptance by peers and the self-esteem that accompanies positive peer interactions are major components of the adolescent's growing sense of autonomy and social identity (Erikson 1959).

Sexuality/Sex–Role Identity

The establishment of a solid sense of sexuality is based on the adolescent's ability to identify with the parent of the same sex and establish a stable, growth-producing relationship with the parent of the opposite sex (Erikson 1963). An age-appropriate interest in or involvement with the opposite sex is generally indicative of positive sexual identity in adolescence (Marcia 1980). An adolescent who feels sexually attractive and comfortable in his or her sexual orientation will experience a heightened sense of adequacy, self-esteem, and independence from infantile objects, all of which combine to form the basis for a solid identity, according to Erikson (1950).

Bourne (1978) suggests that an adolescent's achievement of satisfactory peer relations and especially a mutual heterosexual relationship can provide indirect evidence of intrapsychic separation, one of the identity-mediating processes described in an earlier section. According to Bourne's speculations, such relationships would probably be conflict laden and unstable if the individual is still substantially under the aegis of primitive parental introjections.

School Performance

School performance reveals the presence or absence of feelings of adequacy and mastery in this area of applied skill. According to Eriksonian theory, one of the prerequisites of satisfactory identity formation in adolescence is the sense of industry and mastery attained during the "apprenticeship period" of latency. A successful resolution of the industry vs. inferiority crisis leaves one with a set of basic skills and confidence in one's capacity for worthwhile work (Marcia 1980). In Erikson's terms (1968, 180), the contribution of this stage to ego identity is "the capacity to learn how to be, with skill, what one is in the process of becoming." A sense of industry allows for the possibility of vocational commitment in adolescence. Adolescents who see themselves as deficient may exhibit work paralysis or a sense of futility either in school or on a job.

Self-Image/Self-Esteem

All the theoretical discussions of identity emphasize the importance of the developing sense of self-esteem. Erikson (1959), in particular, notes that

> Self-esteem grows to be a conviction...that one is developing a defined personality within a social reality which one understands. The growing child must at every step derive a vitalizing sense of reality from the awareness that his individual way of mastering experience is a successful variant of the way other people around him master experience and recognize such mastery. (p. 89)

In Erikson's view, the self-esteem attached to ego identity is based on the rudiments of skills and social techniques. It is thus realistically conceived, allowing a growing convergence between ego ideal and social role (Erikson 1959).

ADJUSTMENT AS AN OVERALL MEASURE OF IDENTITY

Erikson (1959) notes that the stabilization of ego identity during adolescence occurs gradually as the individual resynthesizes newly acquired social and vocational roles with other dimensions of the personality. Although Marcia (1966; 1967; 1980) has not directly assessed such global aspects of ego identity as ego synthesis and role stability, Bourne (1978b, 376) claims it is necessary to assume that the adolescent's attainment of stable occupational/ideological commitments is accompanied by increments along these dimensions. He further suggests that "'societal integration,' 'existential self-definition,' 'ego strength,' 'self-cohesiveness,' and, for that matter, 'global adjustment' and 'self esteem,' are perhaps little more than conceptual distinctions reflecting different perspectives or levels of analysis respective to the same reality."

Although research assessing the relationship between identity formation and adjustment has been somewhat limited, existing studies tend to indicate that subjects who have achieved an identity seem less confused in their self-definition and less anxious (two global variables of overall adjustment), according to Marcia (1966). In fact, an overview of the empirical literature on the subject of adjustment as an overall measure of ego identity suggests a rather positive relationship between the two constructs, allowing for its use in the measurement of identity that is employed in this research.

CHAPTER 2

IDENTITY FORMATION IN ADOPTEES: THEORY AND RESEARCH

THERE IS WIDESPREAD DISAGREEMENT as to whether the adopted child is more prone to emotional stress than the non-adopted child. Incidence rates of psychiatric disturbance vary so extensively that it has yet to be determined that adopted children do, in fact, constitute a significant portion of clinic populations. While comparative clinical findings on the adjustment of adoptive children indicate greater incidence of psychiatric disorder (Austad and Simmons 1978; Schecter 1960; Simon and Senturia 1966; Toussieng 1962), nonclinical comparative studies seem to present a less dismal view (Hoopes 1982; Lawder 1969; Witmer 1963). Although data tend to suggest the presence of somewhat greater vulnerability in the adopted child (Hoopes 1982), it is equally apparent that the large majority of adoptees are evidencing a reasonable degree of adjustment. This fact lends support to the conclusion of Goodman and associates (1963) that the higher incidence of adoptees referred for psychiatric treatment has no great social significance. Clearly, more research with normative populations of adoptees is needed.

THE IDENTITY PROCESS IN ADOPTED ADOLESCENTS

The concept of identity, as defined by Erikson and others, has been the prime focus in conceptual discussions of those addressing issues of adjustment in the adopted adolescent. As alluded to in the introduction, a review of the literature on identity formation in adoptees seems to indicate that adolescent identity struggles are adversely affected by the adoptive experience. Statements relating to the intensification of typical adolescent conflicts abound. Frisk (1964), for example, states:

> We must realize that the chances of developing disturbances during adolescence are great in the adopted child. Ego development, identification, and the forming of identity, together with the social environment, are inclined to become complicated. In the course of my studies of the adopted child, it has become apparent that a special problem in the formation of identity has been present. (p. 7)

Similarly, Schoenberg (1974, 549), writing on adoption and identity, asserts that "the creation of families based on psychological, not blood, ties contains inherent identity problems that practice and law seek to mitigate, but can never eliminate."

Psychological Difficulties in the Identity Process

In a well-synthesized discussion of the subject, Sorosky and associates (1975, 24) conclude that "adoptees are *more* [authors' emphasis] vulnerable than the population at large because of the greater likelihood of encountering difficulties in the working through of the psychosexual, psychosocial and psychohistorical aspects of personality development." Four categories of psychological difficulties related to identity conflicts in adoptees have been delineated: (1) disturbances in early object relations; (2) complications in the resolution of the oedipal complex; (3) prolongation of the "family romance" fantasy; and (4) "genealogical bewilderment."

Early Object Relations

Regarding disturbances in the infant's earliest development, Clothier (1943, 223) comments on the loss of fundamental security that distinguishes the adoptee who is deprived of a primitive, nurturant relationship with the biological mother, asserting that "it is to be doubted whether the relationship of the child to its postpartum mother...can be replaced by even the best of substitute mothers." Despite more recent theoretical statements to the contrary (Bowlby 1969), Clothier's comment typifies the unscientific formulations found in the literature on which conceptions of adoptees are still based. Although Bowlby's (1969, XI-XII) extensive work on attachment, for example, has led him to conclude that "what is...essential for mental health is that the infant and young child experience a warm, intimate and continous relationship with his mother *or permanent mother substitute* [author's emphasis] in which both find satisfaction and enjoyment," his formulations have obviously been ignored by most adoption theoreticians.

Schecter (1960) and Simon and Senturia (1966) support Clothier's rather negative view of the potential for greater difficulty in establishing secure and stable early attachments, pointing to the difficulty adoptees have in synthesizing ambivalent feelings for the adoptive parent into a workable, realistic identification. Although Schecter (1960) attributes the aloofness and emotional distance of many adopted children he evaluated to deficiencies in early object relations, some of his clinical examples are open to question, based on the overdetermined nature of much of the symptomatology reported.

Oedipal/Sexual Complications

The issue of oedipal complications and sexual conflicts has been addressed in part by Easson (1973), who refers to difficulties experienced in three related areas of emotional growth that can affect the development of a stable sexual identity in the adopted adolescent: (1) the adolescent's process of emancipation from the adoptive parents; (2) the resolution of incestuous strivings in the adoptive relationship; and (3) the final identification with the parent of the same sex and the concomitant development of mutuality with the opposite sex parent.

As regards the emancipation process, Easson suggests that the longer the youngster delays accepting the adoptive parents with their normal human qualities, the more he or she slows down the necessary preadolescent identification with them and they with him or her, precluding the possibility of the comfortable relationship that is so essential to emancipation. Easson's views are supported by Sokoloff (1977) and Sorosky and associates (1977), who similarly describe exacerbations of the normal dependency-independency conflicts in adopted adolescents, who appear to be more vulnerable to experiences of loss, rejection, and abandonment.

Commenting on the possibility of enhanced incestuous strivings in the families of adopted adolescents where the incest barrier between parent and child or between siblings is "not nearly as strong" as in a blood-related family, Easson (1973) writes:

> In the adopting family, the brothers and sisters can continue a strongly erotic relationship much longer, much more intimately, and with much less anxiety than is possible in a healthy, blood-related family. This unresolved incestuous bond slows down the sexual emancipation of the adopted adolescent and makes it more difficult to develop

appropriate peer sexual relationships outside the family.
(p. 102)

Once again, it is unclear from Easson's statement whether this generalization is based on the norm or the pathological. One need only be reminded of the normal incest taboos that evolve among non-blood-related children of the kibbutz, who grow up together as "brother and sister" with all the repressive phenomena of a blood-related family (Bettelheim 1969). Obviously, incest taboos are not totally dependent on the existence of a blood tie, as Easson seems to suggest.

Regarding the achievement of a satisfactory identification with the same parent, Easson (1973) points to the difficulties inherent in the process for the adopted adolescent who may still want to hold on to glamorous or not-so-glamorous fantasies about the biological parents, which delay acceptance of the adoptive parents and impede a final identification with them. In reviewing some of the intricacies that the oedipal complex poses for the adoptee, Easson (1973, 103) concludes that "the adopted adolescent will reach sex-appropriate adult maturity with more struggle and sometimes after greater delay than in the normal blood-related family." Schecter (1960) concurs, viewing the resolution of the oedipal complex to be so fraught with difficulty that he advises postponing the revelation of the child's adoptive status until after the resolution of the oedipal conflict to avoid complicating this stage of psychosexual development.

The Family Romance

Several theorists (Clothier 1943; Glatzer 1955; Schecter 1960; Simon and Senturia 1966) have postulated a prolongation and reinforcement of the family romance fantasy in adopted children that impedes the adolescent's identification with the adoptive parent. The family romance fantasy refers to that brief state in normal child development in which children experience doubt about their "natural-born" status, often believing they are adopted. The fantasy develops as a result of children's inability to tolerate ambivalent feelings toward the parental figures, enabling them to ameliorate real or imagined disappointments within the parental relationship by imagining something better. For the adopted child, the fantasy appears more attainable and thus interferes with its intended function of mastery, impeding the identification process as a whole (Clothier 1943; Wieder 1977a). In an excellent discussion of the family romance fantasy and the adopted child, Lawton and Gross (1964), however, caution those who attribute a universality to the family romance as a source of specific problems for the adopted child. They believe that the prolongation of the family romance and its fixation in the adopted child results when certain adoptive parents drive their children to open rejection and stimulate comparisons with the biological parents.

Genealogical Problems

Lastly, the issue of genealogical bewilderment has been discussed at great length by many writers who echo Clothier's (1943) sentiments that the lack of racial antecedents lies at the core of what is unique to the psychology of the adopted child. The term itself was coined by Sants (1964), who described a state of confusion and uncertainty in a child who either has no knowledge of his biological parents or only uncertain knowledge of them. Sants felt that this state of uncertainty could fundamentally undermine the child's security and result in the development of an insecure self-image and confused sense of identity in adolescence. Sants discusses the problems engendered by different heredities in adoptive families, explaining how differences in appearance and/or intellectual skills can severely hamper an adoptive child's capacity to identify with the adoptive parents, impeding a sense of belonging and the security that accompanies it.

Others (Frisk 1964; Wieder 1978) also have concluded that the adopted adolescent's identity formation is impaired because an essential part of himself or herself has been cut off and remains unknown. All these writers are obviously echoing Erikson's belief in the importance of having an unbroken genetic and historical attachment to the past, present, and future in the process of identity consolidation. Wieder (1978), like Sants (1964), discusses how the lack of a "blood line" complicates the process of identity consolidation by the absence of "biological mutuality" in adoptive families. In his discussion on when and whether to disclose the adoption status, Wieder (1978) mentions that children from adoptive families frequently refer to their obvious lack of mutual family features. The absence of biological mutuality can create difficulties in the identification process as Sants (1964) previously indicated, leaving the youngster with feelings of "differentness" that aggravate the ongoing attempts at personality integration.

Frisk (1964), in dealing with the genealogical problem from a slightly different perspective, has described how the lack of family background knowledge in the adolescent adoptee prevents the development of a healthy "genetic ego," which is then replaced by a "hereditary ghost." Since the genetic ego is obscure, the adolescent has no way of knowing what might be passed on to the next generation. Furthermore, the adolescent's knowledge that the biological parents were unable to look after him or her is interpreted as proof of the biological parents' inferiority, giving rise to fears of hereditary psychical abnormalities that can lower self-esteem (Frisk 1964).

In sum, the literature reviewed on the identity process in adoptees seems to present a rather compelling view of the stresses that adoptive status brings to the ongoing attempts at identity resolution in adolescence. Again, it is important to bear in mind that the foregoing discussion is theoretically based, with the preponderance of conclusions drawn from the clinical data of writers who have attempted to account for the existence of pathology in their clinical patients. What appear to be missing up to this point are any attempts to tie these theoretical formulations to empirical study of a nonclinical nature where the emphasis on normality might provide a less biased view.

FACTORS THAT ENHANCE OR IMPEDE IDENTITY RESOLUTION IN ADOPTED ADOLESCENTS

Several related factors have been noted in the literature as enhancing or impeding identity resolution in adopted adolescents. These are (1) family relationships; (2) communication about adoption; (3) parental attitudes about adoption; (4) the impact of "telling about adoption"; and (5) miscellaneous issues.

Family Relationships

With regard to the first factor, the relevance of family relationships, Glatzer (1955, 56), in an early paper on adoption and delinquency, emphasized the significance of a good object relationship between the adopted child and his parents in the prevention of pathology. McWhinnie (1969, 138) likewise attributed an adolescent's positive attitude toward adoption to a solid relationship with the adoptive parents. She mentioned that well-adjusted teenagers evidenced a loving relationship with the parents. Conversely, poorly adjusted teenagers showed signs of "marked ambivalence, of excessive devotion, coupled with resentment that they were thus tied by conscience and feelings of duty." In studies reviewing cases of adolescent adoptees coming to the attention of mental health practitioners or the courts, Barinbaum (1974), Goodman and Magno-Nora (1975), Rickarby and Egan (1980), and Sabalis and Burch (1980) similarly conclude that it is the quality of parenting rather than adoption per se that plays the significant role in causing the adjustment problems of adopted individuals.

Communication About Adoption

Many writers have addressed the importance of openness in communication about issues of adoption (Blum 1976; Schoenberg 1974; Sokoloff 1977; Sorosky et al. 1977). Sorosky and Sokoloff (1977, 977) both agree that "the more open the communication about all adoption related matters, the less likely the adolescent will have to resort to excessive fantasizing or acting out in an attempt to fill in identity lacunae." Writing on identity problems in adoptees, Schoenberg (1974) advocates bringing the fact of adoptive status into the open, thereby encouraging a social climate of lessened discomfort about adoptive status. In a similar fashion, Blum (1976) advises that the parent of an adopted adolescent be as open and nondefensive as possible to questions concerning the child's heritage. Although openness of communication obviously enhances adjustment, McWhinnie (1969) warns that too much talk about adoption can be detrimental, especially if parental discussions do not coincide with the children's feelings and needs.

Parental Attitudes About Adoption

Parental attitudes about adoption have been shown to influence the adolescent's achievement of a healthy sense of identity. McWhinnie (1969, 134) found that the comfort level of adoptive parents played a role in the adjustment of the adolescent. She suggests that parental discomfort in discussion of adoption "relates to doubts about their adequacy as parents, their fear that their children will love them less if they know they are not biologically their own children and concern that they may seek out their 'other mother.'" Blum (1976) also noted that for the insecure adoptive parent, conversations about genealogy were fraught with feelings of rejection and guilt that could only intensify the adolescent's struggle with identity-related issues. She concluded that parental attitudes reinforced by feelings of inadequacy could do much to influence the child's negative self-image. Schecter (1960) observed that adoptive mothers in his clinical caseload often presented intense feelings of inadequacy regarding their child-bearing functions, an attitude that contributed to their tendency toward overprotectiveness and difficulties with issues of independence.

Critical attitudes of adoptive parents toward the biological parents can also interfere with the adolescent's identity process. Frisk (1964) indicated that unfavorable reports about biological parents gave rise to identity problems in adolescent adoptees, who interpreted these reports as proof of their own genetic inferiority. Rickarby and Egan (1980) found that notions of "genetic inferiority" arose in response to parents' attempts to mitigate their own feelings of guilt and inadequacy in relationship struggles with their adopted adolescents. According to Blum (1976) and Nospitz (1979), the criticism adoptive parents sometimes level at biological parents tends to impede a positive identification with the fantasied biological parent.

Blum (1976) suggests that the need of the adoptive parent to downgrade the biological parent tends to reflect feelings of insecurity or the lack of feelings of entitlement as a parent. The "negative identity" that results often leads to social deviation or delinquency, according to McWhinnie (1969, 135), who noted that "where adoptive mothers feared that their adolescent daughters would inherit instability or immoral behavioral patterns from their biological mothers, their mistrusting behavior toward these adolescents drove them into behaving in just the way that their mothers feared." McWhinnie (1969, 141) concludes that "the aim must be to help the inquiring adolescent…to learn of his biological parentage in a positive, acceptable and undamaging way, emphasizing what is known of the positive attributes of his natural parents and encouraging consideration of what may have been the difficulties in their human condition."

Both Frisk (1964) and Sorosky and associates (1977) comment on the oversensitivity of adoptive parents to their adolescents' strivings for independence. Frisk believes that the parents' overreaction to insignificant relational phenomena is attributable to feelings of inferiority originating from their incapacity to bear children. Sorosky (1977, 55) similarly suggests that adoptive parents tend to "view any disengagement from themselves as an abandonment and a return to the lonely, insecure feelings associated with the preadoption childless period." He points out that this may result in infantilization of the adolescent and thus prevent an emerging individuation. In these cases, Sorosky notes, the adolescent is often pushed into a state of rebellion to preserve his or her sense of integrity.

As a final note on the subject of parental attitudes, Kirk (1964) described a tendency on the part of some adoptive parents to deny the basic differences (inability to conceive biologically) that originally created the need for adoption. He felt that the coping mechanisms of "rejecting difference" could result in poorer communication within the family and prevent a healthy adaptation for all family members. Sorosky and associates (1977, 65) concur with Kirk's statement, concluding that "the healthiest adaptation occurs when the adoptive parents have been reasonably successful in resolving their feelings about infertility and are willing to acknowledge that their role is different…than that of biological parents."

The Impact of "Telling About Adoption"

The question of whether to disclose adoption status has been argued to some extent in the literature. Goodman and Magno-Nora (1975) present an "empirical" argument for withholding information of biological origins in their study of court-referred vs. parent-referred adolescent adoptees, citing a positive correlation between incidence of "runaway" in the court-referred group and the dissemination of information given about biological origins. Goodman and Magno-Nora suggest that the higher incidence of runaway reflected impairment in the adolescent's perceived basic security. Although weakened family cohesion and other signs of family dysfunction were noted in the two groups, Goodman and Magno-Nora seem inclined to attribute the sense of insecurity in these disturbed adolescents to disclosure of adoption status rather than to family factors, a conclusion that seems questionable to the authors. Goodman's and Magno-Nora's study is not the first that has based generalizations about adoptive practice on conclusions drawn from a psychiatric population.

Sants (1964) has argued to the contrary, that a youngster be told not only of the adoption but also the facts of his or her origins, indicating that family secrets about heredity are more disturbing than reality to healthy identity formation. McWhinnie (1969) has similarly advocated disclosure, especially by the adoptive parents, as disclosure from an outside source was found to cause resentment and lasting emotional trauma in adolescents. This stance has since been adopted by the Committee on Adoption of the American Academy of Pediatrics.

Perhaps an even more compelling debate than the question of whether to disclose adoption status concerns the issue of when to tell a child. Wieder (1977a, b; 1978) has been the most prolific writer on the deleterious emotional effects of telling children under 3 years of age. He sharply criticizes the prevailing practice of early disclosure, commenting that telling too early leads to disturbances in object relationships, cognitive function, and fantasy life in his patients. Wieder (1978, 796) found that "immaturity and the inability to clearly comprehend or master the implications of the communication produced confusion, overwhelming anxiety, shame and rage, leaving lasting effects on the adoptee's personality and intellect." According to Wieder, all of his patients who were told early experienced the disclosure as a shaming rejection by the adoptive mother. In addition, each patient reacted to the knowledge of being adopted as if it were a narcissistic injury, producing damage to self-esteem.

Wieder's (1977a, b; 1978) sentiments are generally consonant with Schecter's (1960) original comments on disclosure. Schecter, as stated earlier, advises postponing the revelation of the child's adoptive status until after the resolution of the oedipal conflict (roughly 6 years) to avoid complications in the identification process. Wieder (1978, 796) uses his clinical data on analytic patients to conclude that "early disclosure is traumatic and disruptive to the developing personality," especially in light of the general discovery that all his patients had wished they had not been told early. The tendency to draw conclusions for general practice from clinical data is again apparent and open to question.

Lawton and Gross (1964) suggest that parents should answer questions about a child's origins as directly and simply as possible during the preschool and early childhood years, just as they would about sex. Perhaps Nospitz's

(1979, 343) reminder that "telling is a gradual process of communication over time" is most noteworthy. He indicates that at every stage in the adopted child's development, fantasies about adoption will vary, as will the type of assistance needed.

More recent cognitive research on adoption revelation has amplified Nospitz's comments on process. Brodzinsky and associates (1980, 1981) have emphasized the importance of disclosing age-appropriate adoption information based on an understanding of the child's constructivistic process of knowledge acquisition. They have stressed the importance of knowing what the child's cognitive capabilities and limitations are before disseminating information on adoption; by taking these cognitive factors into account, parents can truly enhance their child's ability to cope with the adoptive status.

The authors tend to agree with the view upheld by Lawton and Gross (1964) and others (Glatzer 1955; Sorosky et al. 1977) who contend that it is not the timing of disclosure that is significant but the context in which the disclosure takes place. Lawton and Gross (1964), for example, suggest that if reasonably secure adoptive parents disclose information in an anxiety-free context, no negative consequences need occur. Trauma from disclosure at age 3 to 6 "is but a complex function of pervasive interrelationships among the family members," according to Lawton and Gross (1964, 641). Glatzer (1955) and Sorosky and associates (1977) concur with Lawton's view, citing the importance of good relationships between adopted children and their parents as a primary factor in successful disclosure.

Miscellaneous Issues

Four additional factors have been cited in the literature as influential in the adaptation of the adopted youngster. The first pertains to the issue of early placement. Clothier (1943) has indicated that if placement has occurred in earliest infancy, there is the maximum probability that the child's overall development will parallel that of a nonadopted child. She states:

> The child who is permanently placed within the first month
> or two of life may be influenced in the roots of his personal-
> ity by his adoptive family. His primary identifications will be
> with his adoptive mother and father. The earlier in life a
> child becomes a part of a family, the more deeply can that
> family become a part of that child. (p. 224)

Problems of "mismatch" have also been mentioned as contributory to adjustment difficulties in adoptive children. Nospitz (1979) notes, for example, that children available for adoption often have average intellectual skills compared to the above-average intellects of their adoptive parents. This discrepancy may prove to be disappointing to the parents and frustrating for the child who is eager to please and obtain the approval and acceptance that he or she needs. Mismatch issues may be exacerbated by extreme differences in appearance or temperament as well, not unlike those difficulties that arise in biological families when temperamental differences between parent and child exist, as Thomas and associates (1968) have shown.

Another factor that has received somewhat less attention but appears to contribute significantly to adjustment difficulty is family composition. It has been mentioned by McWhinnie (1967), particularly as regards sibling interaction problems in adoptive families, and more recently by Hoopes (1982), who found that "mixed families" (i.e., families with both adoptive and biological siblings) have more difficulty in the area of parental functioning and maintenance of overall self-esteem than do adoptive, nonmixed families.

Finally, the presence of neurodevelopmental problems in an adopted child may place the child and the family in jeopardy, according to Taichert and Harvin (1975). Subtle learning and behavioral problems that can undermine any family's functioning may lead to "tragic family dysfunction" in light of the additional stresses that adoptive status imposes in these families.

In summary, all the factors mentioned above appear to have significant impact on the identity-formation process of adoptees. The current study affords an attempt to test the validity of these ideas empirically.

SEARCH BEHAVIOR AND IDENTITY FORMATION
IN THE ADOPTED ADOLESCENT

As the adopted child enters adolescence, he or she becomes more acutely aware of the biological link of the generations (Blum 1976). One need only recall Erikson's (1959) definition of identity to know how essential to the process of identity formation is the presence of unbroken historical connections to the past, present, and future. As both Sants (1964) and Frisk (1964) have indicated, the identity conflicts of many adolescent adoptees are intensified by the knowledge of having genetic links to hereditary "unknowns." The adoptees' "dual identity" problem may prompt them to search out their past and pursue information about this unknown self in an effort to resolve the break in the continuity of their lives.

Controversy as to the extent of curiosity that adoptees manifest about their genealogical background has continued, although all theorists tend to agree that the adolescent's identity concerns intensify his or her interest in this area (Sorosky 1975). Some authors contend that the adolescent's concern about genealogy is common to all adoptees and is not a sign of emotional disturbance or family conflict (Blum 1976; Kirk 1966; McWhinnie 1969; Schecter et al. 1964). Nospitz (1979), for example, claims that the adopted adolescent's increased interest in his or her biological parents occurs in the normal process of separating from one's parents and seeking the roots on which to build an identity.

Many different theories have been proposed to explain the intensification of "search behavior" in some adolescents, although actual search behavior has not been consistently differentiated in the literature from "intense curiosity." Some theorists have suggested that curiosity and search behavior are greatest in adoptive homes in which there has been a strained relationship and difficulty in communicating openly about the adoption situation (Clothier 1943; McWhinnie 1969; Triseliotis 1973). Clothier (1943), for example, suggests that the need of the child to know about the biological parents may vary with the lack of positive identification with the adoptive parents. McWhinnie (1969) similarly concluded, from her retrospective study, that the more secure and happily accepted the adopted child feels within the adoptive family, the less will be the need to search out origins. In a retrospective study of 70 adult adoptees, Triseliotis (1973) found that the greater the dissatisfaction with the adoptive family relationship and with themselves, the greater the possibility that adoptees would seek a reunion with the biological parents, whereas the better the image of themselves and of their adoptive parents, the greater the likelihood that they would merely seek background information. Other studies by Sorosky and associates (1975) have proposed that an adolescent adoptee's genealogical concerns and search efforts are more reflective of innate personality traits, such as inquisitiveness and curiosity, and are less dependent on the nature of the adoptive family relationship.

Not all adoptees, however, want to search. Ambivalence about searching is apparently common, according to the American Academy of Pediatrics' Committee on Adoption (1971). Even Frisk (1964) noted that although some adoptees experienced the need to investigate their genetic background, they were at the same time afraid of not being able to integrate it intrapsychically. Blum (1976, 247) has indicated that "sometimes adequate information is all the adoptee is seeking and this, openly shared, can make the search for the actual parent unnecessary." Wieder (1978) corroborated Blum's findings with clinical data that showed that analysis of the wish to search revealed it to be a wish to know about, not to rejoin, the biological parents. McWhinnie (1969) similarly found that although many adoptees retrospectively spoke of wanting to meet their biological parents out of curiosity, they were emphatic about not wishing these parents to know who they were—that is, they would have liked to observe their biological parents without being observed in return.

Some sex differences in curiosity and search behavior have been noted in the literature. McWhinnie (1969), for example, found that adolescent boys in her study tended to be less curious about their biological parents than adolescent girls. Farber (1977) likewise noted in her observations of 19 adopted children that girls tended to manifest greater interest, involvement, and conflict with regard to adoption than did boys. She wondered whether this heightened curiosity and interest in searching was related to a girl's investment in reproductive concerns, which would be a significant part of the normative feminine identification process. Personal communication from an adoption worker at the Children's Bureau of Wilmington, Delaware, supported these findings, in that a higher incidence of female adolescents in her caseload expressed interest in searching for their biological parents.*

In summary, most of the literature on search behavior consists of formulations based on clinical observations of a limited number of cases, or investigations of adult adoptees. Although there is an abundance of theories about why some adolescents search, few theorists have based their assumptions on actual empirical studies of adolescents. Not only have differences in expressed curiosity and actual search attempts been blurred, as noted earlier, but at times there seems to be a lack of theoretical consistency in references to the timing of adolescence. As Lawton and Gross (1964) and Wieder (1978) have said, research is urgently needed to clarify the remaining questions.

Only two studies have attempted to compare an adopted and non-adopted adolescent population on identity-related issues. In a comparison of self-concept in 18- to 25-year-old nonclinical adoptees and nonadoptees, Norvell and Guy (1977) found no significant difference between the two groups, using the Berger Self-Concept Scale. In fact, the adoptive group obtained slightly higher mean scores. On the basis of these results, they concluded that adoptive status alone cannot produce a negative identity and suggested that other factors, such as quality of parent-child interaction, are perhaps more pertinent to successful adjustment in adoption cases.

More recently, Simmons (1980) studied identity formation in 18- to 30-year-old adopted and nonadopted subjects, using a nonclinical population of each. Various scales, including the California Psychological Inventory, the Tennessee Self-Concept Scale, and the Adjective Check List, were used to measure dimensions of identity. Simmons found significant differences between the two groups, indicating that adoptees were less well socialized, tended to be more impulsive and demanding, and had lower self-esteem. His results were interpreted as supporting the hypothesis that adoptees have more difficulty forming a sense of identity than nonadoptees, thus contradicting the findings of Norvell and Guy (1977).

---

*Personal communication with Kit Angell, Clinical Social Worker, Wilmington, Delaware, May 1982.

Both studies, however, raise questions on two counts. First, the age range of their samples exceeds the period of adolescence commonly defined by such writers on adolescence as Erikson (1950) and Blos (1970). One would be hard pressed to generalize their results to a sample of senior high school students, whose identity formation would tend to reflect a less consolidated stage of the process. Second, and perhaps more significant, is the fact that both studies have limited the measurement of identity to self-report inventories, thus giving a rather superficial index of a highly complex construct.

The current study is an effort to amplify knowledge about the impact of adoption on the adolescent's emotional adjustment as measured by an assessment of ego identity. Although an extensive body of literature already exists on the comparative adjustment of adoptive children through the age of 15 (Hoopes et al. 1970; Hoopes 1982), considerably less is known about what happens to 15- to 18-year-old adoptees. Most of the current theoretical literature on identity formation in the adoptee suggests that adoptive status adversely affects an adolescent's consolidation of ego identity. The purpose of this study is to test this empirically, with the added hope of identifying factors that enhance or impede resolution of identity issues in the adolescent adoptee. This research intends to provide a systematic, empirical examination of theoretical assumptions in the literature that have heretofore shaped much of the current thinking on adoption outcome.

The use of a normative sample of high school students can, it is hoped, extend the ability to generalize from statements that have for the most part emanated from clinical data, and consequently have been highly speculative and limited in applicability. The additional emphasis on search behavior in adolescent adoptees is intended to answer questions on this affect-laden topic, specifically in relation to what differentiates the genealogically curious from those who are not. Data on this subject could have broad implications for clinical practice and preventive work with adopted adolescents. In the present research, the measurement of ego identity is approached through both psychosocial and self-report indices, which, when combined, may offer a deeper look at adjustment in adolescence.

QUESTIONS TO BE EXPLORED

This study was designed to explore the following questions raised by the literature regarding the adolescent adoptee:

1. Does adoptive status affect an adolescent's process of identity formation? More specifically, are there significant differences in ego identity between adopted and nonadopted 15- to 18-year-olds drawn from a nonclinical population?

Given the overwhelming amount of both theoretical and clinical observations that stress the special identity problems of the adopted adolescent, one might expect to see differences in functioning between the adoptive and nonadoptive groups.

2.   What are the family variables that enhance or impede the development of ego identity in the adopted adolescent? Three major variables were selected for study, based on the literature that points to the relevance of family functioning in the overall adjustment of the adopted adolescent (McWhinnie 1969; Schoenberg 1974; Sorosky et al. 1977).

The first family variable explored was style of family interaction, specifically regarding communication about adoption. For instance, does perceived ease of communication about adoption within the family predict successful identity formation in the adopted adolescent? One would expect that a generally open, easy interactional style between parents and child would promote a sense of comfort about the issue of adoption, as it is axiomatic that a child's relationship to his or her parents influences the way in which the child is given and reacts to information (Wieder 1978). It was predicted that the style of communication about adoption as perceived by the adolescent will significantly affect the youngster's ability to cope with adoptive status and with the identity tasks of adolescence. That is, adopted subjects in families that communicate openly about adoption should manifest higher levels of ego identity than adopted subjects from families in which the issue is closed.

The second family variable considered was the quality of family relationships and interaction, since much of the current literature on identity formation in adopted adolescents speaks to the importance of this variable as a determinant of positive ego identity. It was thought that adoptees who manifest good relationships with their adoptive parents should reveal higher levels of identity formation than adoptees whose parental relationships are less than satisfactory.

The third family variable studied was family composition, as defined by the presence or absence of nonadopted siblings within the adoptive family. The authors wished to explore the impact of family composition on the adjustment of adolescent adoptees. Both theoretical and empirical writings have suggested that adopted youngsters encounter more difficulties when nonadopted children are present in the family (Hoopes 1982). It was predicted, therefore, that adopted adolescents in families with nonadopted siblings are at higher risk of difficulties in identity formation than those with all adopted siblings.

3.   What can be said about the presence or absence of search behavior in the adolescent adoptee? More specifically, is there some relationship between search behavior and

identity formation in this group? The existence of search efforts in adoptees has generated considerable speculation as to whether this behavior relates to the quality of the adoptive relationship and self-image of the adoptee (Triseliotis 1973) or whether its manifestation is simply related to curiosity stemming from the adoption issue in general (Schecter et al. 1964). Search behavior is defined as an adolescent's active and persistent effort to obtain information about the biological parents. It was hypothesized that a relationship does, in fact, exist between search behavior and the degree of identity consolidation present in the adolescent adoptee, and that this relationship may be curvilinear: that is, evidence of this behavior would be found more pervasively in adolescents who score at the extreme ends on a measure of ego identity, thus manifesting either prominent signs of consolidation or marked diffusion in identity.

It was believed that adolescents who were more secure in their definition of self, on the one hand, would be less vulnerable to the effect of information about their origins and therefore more curious—they would search. On the other hand, adolescents with little sense of "who they are" might likewise attempt to search, hoping that information about their origins would serve to consolidate their fragmented or poorly defined sense of identity.

4. What specific variables influence the presence of search behavior in adoptees? This study examined the relationship between search efforts and perceived style of communication about adoption in an effort to ascertain whether Triseliotis's (1973) retrospective findings on adult adoptees apply to an adolescent population. It was assumed that adolescent adoptees from families in which the style of communication about adoption is open would be less inclined to search.

Finally, the study examined the impact of family composition on the presence of search behavior. It was thought that adopted adolescents with nonadopted siblings would search more frequently because of the added stress imposed by their family composition.

CHAPTER 3

METHODS AND PROCEDURES

THE SAMPLE FOR THIS STUDY consisted of a total of 91 white adolescents (50 adopted and 41 nonadopted), ranging in age from 15 to 18, inclusive. All of the subjects were senior high school students drawn from 10th, 11th, and 12th grades, with the preponderance of subjects (97.8%) from the 11th and 12th grades. Both adoptive and nonadoptive participants were of at least average intelligence and were assumed to fall within the normal range of adjustment. Although contact with a mental health practitioner did not automatically eliminate a subject (as it was assumed that therapeutic contact would randomize throughout both groups), any adolescent with either severe psychopathology or known retardation was excluded from the final sample. The subjects of both groups were rather evenly divided by gender, with a mean age of 16.6 years.

ADOPTIVE SAMPLE

The adoptive group was obtained from the original population of families comprising the Delaware Family Study, a longitudinal adoption study begun in 1962. Any family with an adolescent between the ages of 15½ and 18 from the Pennsylvania, New Jersey, and Delaware area was invited to participate in this final phase of research for the Delaware Family Study Project. Letters were sent to the parents and teenagers of 90 such families, and 50 adolescents volunteered.

The 50 adoptive volunteers were all white, representing families with a range of socioeconomic status and educational levels, although the majority reflected the original adoptive population of largely middle-class families of professional or corporate occupations (Hollingshead 1957). All the adopted youngsters in this sample had been placed with their parents before the age of 24 months by the Children's Bureau of Wilmington, Delaware. The majority (70%) were placed between the ages of 10 and 60 weeks. For a more detailed description of the original Delaware Family Study population see Hoopes (1982).

The present adoptive sample consisted of two groups of adoptees: a group of 39 adolescents with one or more adopted siblings and a "mixed" group of 11 adolescents with nonadopted siblings. Ninety-two percent of all adoptive subjects came from intact families.

COMPARISON SAMPLE

The nonadoptive comparison group consisted of 41 adolescents drawn from two suburban high school populations that approximated that of the adoptive group. Two of the 41 came from the original reference group of biological children of the Delaware Family Study. The remaining 39 were volunteers who responded to an announcement about the study that was read in the 11th and 12th grade homerooms of both schools. The comparison group was matched as closely as possible for age, sex, grade, socioeconomic status, religious affiliation, sibling number, birth order, family structure (intactness vs. separation, divorce or remarriage). Only two significant differences between the adoptive and comparison groups were noted: number of siblings and birth order of the targeted adolescent. The nonadoptive subjects came from families with a somewhat larger number of siblings, as might be anticipated, thus allowing for greater range in birth order. Although not statistically significant, it is noted that 19.5% of comparison subjects versus 8% of adoptive families came from families of divorce, separation, or remarriage.

PROCEDURES AND INSTRUMENTATION

All the subjects in the study were interviewed individually. Interviews were conducted at either the Children's Bureau of Wilmington, Delaware, Bryn Mawr College's Child Study Institute, or within the guidance departments of two suburban high schools. All the locations contained standard private offices with desks and chairs for interviewing. Interview sessions lasted approximately one hour, with some as long as an hour and a half, depending on the loquaciousness of the subject. Subjects were told that "this is a study on how kids from different types of families think and feel about things important in the life of a teenager." Adopted subjects were additionally informed that some of the interview questions had to do with their thoughts and feelings about being adopted. The subjects were encouraged to be as open and honest in their communications as they could, and confidentiality was guaranteed. Adolescents were assured that none of the information obtained would be shared with either parents, officials of the Children's Bureau (in the case of an adopted subject), or school personnel (in the case of a nonadopted subject).

Three dependent measures (the Tan Ego Identity Scale, the Offer Self-Image Questionnaire for Adolescents, and a Semistructured Interview) were selected to assess dimensions of ego identity as defined earlier in this study. Another measure (the Social Atom task), though not specific to ego identity, was devised to complement the three identity instruments by providing a somewhat more unstructured means of capturing some relevant aspects of the psychological world of the adolescent.

1.   The interview session itself began with a *demographic information sheet* that was filled out by the interviewer. Subjects were asked for certain identifying information, including other persons in the household, birth status of siblings, and changes in family status over the last 5 years.

2.   A modified *Social Atom* task followed (appendix A). Subjects were given a pencil and blank sheet of paper and were told to list the names (limit of 10) of the most socially or emotionally significant persons in their lives. When subjects were finished, they were asked to rate on a 0-to-5 influence scale (using 0 to represent the lowest amount of influence) each person listed. "Influence" was defined as the ability of a significant person to change how a subject might think or feel. When this part of the task was completed, subjects were given another piece of paper with a dot in the center representing themselves. Using dots to represent the significant persons already listed, they were then asked to place each person in relation to the center dot according to the degree of felt intimacy between themselves and that person.

Finally, when the task was completed, adopted subjects were asked whether they might want to place their biological parents in their Social Atom (if excluded). Average time for this task was 5 to 10 minutes.

The modified Social Atom task was included among the dependent measures as a nonverbal, less structured means of assessing and amplifying some of the relationship factors that were tapped in the Semistructured Interview. The Social Atom, conceived by Moreno (1953), is a sociometric device that allows for the systematic measurement of interpersonal relationships and networks. It was selected to supplement the more direct self-report data, thereby diminishing the intrusion of social desirability factors. Its spatial dimension afforded an opportunity to glean information about the adolescent's interpersonal world that might or might not be attainable through a verbal medium. It was hoped that this measure might therefore augment the validity and reliability of the data obtained from the other instruments in the study.

Eleven Social Atom variable scores, enumerated below, were obtained for all subjects:

1. Total number of persons in the Social Atom
2. Number of "category" types (e.g., mother; father; same sex peers; opposite sex peers; relatives [siblings, grandparents, extended family], and nonfamily adults)
3. Influence score for mother
4. Influence score for father
5. Total influence score for parents
6. Total influence score for same sex peers
7. Total influence score for opposite sex peers
8. Total number of same sex peers
9. Total number of opposite sex peers
10. Category containing the single highest influence score (parent only; peer only; parent and peer; other category or combination)
11. Category of those members of the Social Atom falling closest to the center dot (self), defined by the two closest dots to the self (parent only; peer only; parent and peer; other category or combination)

Several assumptions directed the choice of these particular variables for study. Based on the theoretical notions of Erikson (1959) and Blos (1967), who have addressed the object relational processes in adolescence, the following assumptions were made: (a) adolescents with an extremely limited social network would be less well adjusted than those with a more expansive or varied network of significant others; (b) adolescents who totally omit either peers or parents from their Social Atom (or whose influence scores for either group is zero) would likely be less adaptive than those with influential representatives from each of these two groups; (c) adolescents with both same and opposite sex peers represented in their Social Atom would tend to be better adjusted than those who include only one of these two groups. Clearly, with the process of separation-individuation in adolescence, one would anticipate an expansion in social network to include a peer group, though not to the total exclusion of parental figures as anchors in the adolescent's relational system.

3. The *Semistructured Interview* followed next. Subjects were informed that they would be asked for their opinions on many topics that teenagers normally consider. Certain adolescents chose to elaborate spontaneously on their answers, extending the interview time. However, the average time spent on the task was approximately 25 minutes.

The Interview was designed for this study to tap aspects of the adolescent's functioning pertinent to identity formation. It was included as a means of providing a deeper psychosocial experience, congruent with Erikson's

(1950, 1959) and Marcia's (1966) formulation of identity as a psychosocial task. Its intent was to enrich the self-report measures by providing a phenomenological account of how adolescents view themselves in different contexts. Subjects were encouraged to elaborate upon their answers.

This instrument is subdivided into five sections, the first of which contains questions relating solely to adoption, administered to the adoptive group only. The remaining four sections include questions grouped around those behavioral correlates of adolescent identity that were outlined earlier: (a) family relatedness, (b) peer relations, (c) school performance, and (d) self-esteem. The interview contains a built-in rating scale (1 to 3) for the majority of the items, allowing raw score subtotals for the four dimensions: family, peers, school, and self-esteem. A total raw score provides an overall measure of adjustment, with higher scores indicating better adjustment. (See appendix B.)

4.   The session ended with two paper and pencil tasks, each with instructions printed on the instruments themselves. The subjects were asked to fill them out in as forthright a fashion as possible. The first, the *Offer Self-Image Questionnaire for Adolescents*, was a questionnaire that took approximately 15 minutes to complete; the second (the *Tan Ego Identity Scale*) was a brief "opinion scale" averaging about 5 minutes. While the subjects completed these tasks, the experimenter transcribed all qualitative remarks that were of potential interest to the study.

The Offer Self-Image Questionnaire (OSIQ) (Offer 1973) was selected as a self-report measure of psychological well-being and adjustment of the teenager. It is a well-standardized, self-descriptive personality test for adolescent boys and girls between the ages of 13 and 19, yielding adjustment scores in 11 areas of functioning grouped into 5 aspects of the self-system (psychological, social, family, sexual, and coping), reflecting many of the components of ego identity delineated in the theoretical writings of Erikson (1950), Mahler and associates (1975), and Blos (1967).

The Tan Ego Identity Scale (Tan et al. 1977) was chosen on Marcia's recommendation* for use as a short objective measure of overall ego identity as defined by Erikson (1950, 1959). The measure consists of 12 paired items each with two response options: one response reflects ego identity achievement, the other, identity diffusion. This particular ego identity scale was purported to be free of response set contamination, a criticism of several previous measures of ego identity.

---

*As conveyed in a personal communication with James Marcia, Professor of Psychology, Simon Fraser University, British Columbia, Canada.

CHAPTER 4

RESULTS AND DISCUSSION

UPON EXAMINATION of the mean scores and standard deviations on the three dependent measures of ego identity for all subjects, one may conclude that the adolescents in this study appear to be rather well adjusted as a group, showing signs of appropriate functioning in all spheres of their life (table 1). There are no substantive extremes in any of the personality dimensions that would indicate deviant personality patterns. These results seem to corroborate the findings of Offer and associates (1981) that indicated "normal" or typical adolescents had basically positive psychological self-images and family relationships, saw themselves as sociable and confident in their future social and vocational roles, were not afraid of their sexuality, and seemed able to face life situations with little fear and with a reasonable amount of self-confidence. Results thus confirm that the sample selected for study falls within the average range of adjustment, suggesting a truly representative nonclinical population of adolescents.

Intercorrelations of the dependent ego identity measures revealed significant relationships both within and between the various measures in the expected directions (table 2). A positive relationship between overall ego identity (Tan Ego Identity Scale) and self-esteem (OSIQ Overall Average Self Score) was noted, thus corroborating theoretical statements of such a connection posited by Erikson (1959) and Blos (1962, 1970). Somewhat more impressive were the correlations between the Interview subfactors and the OSIQ Overall Average Self Score, suggesting that the various Interview subfactors were, in fact, significantly related to the OSIQ. This finding lends validity to the Interview as a measure of adjustment in adolescents.

TABLE 1
Mean Scores and Standard Deviations on Ego Identity Measures
for All Subjects ($N = 91$)

Dependent Measure*	Mean	S.D.	Range	Possible Range Low High
Tan Ego Identity Scale	7.91	1.63	8	0 – 12
Interview Total Score	72.47	6.72	33	30 – 88
Family Factor	27.60	3.82	17	11 – 33
Peer Factor	21.68	2.27	11	9 – 25
School Factor	9.31	2.30	8	4 – 12
Self-Esteem Factor	13.86	1.89	11	6 – 18
Offer Self-Image Questionnaire (OSIQ)				
Overall Average Self Score	52.37	10.79		
Psychological Self Score	52.35	12.56		
Social Self Score	51.76	12.40		
Sexual Self Score	46.71	14.91		
Family Self Score	52.17	13.33		
Coping Self Score	53.91	12.62		

*All scores except for OSIQ are reported as raw scores. Scores on the OSIQ have been converted to scale scores with a mean scale score of 50 and a standard deviation of 15.

MAJOR FINDINGS

Do Significant Differences Exist Between Adopted and Nonadopted Adolescents?

It was hypothesized that adopted subjects might obtain lower scores on measures of identity formation and adjustment than might nonadopted adolescents. A comparison of adopted and nonadopted subjects on all three dependent measures of ego identity is reported in table 3. Contrary to expectation, significant differences were not found in the expected direction between the two groups. More specifically, adopted subjects showed no deficits in functioning on measures of overall identity when compared to their nonadopted counterparts. In fact, higher scores on one of the identity measures (Tan Ego Identity Scale) were obtained by the adoptive group ($F = 4.05; p \leq .05$). These results were consistent with Norvell and Guy's (1977) findings of no significant difference between adopted and nonadopted subjects for self-concept, though they contradict Simmons's (1980) conclusions. There were no indications that the present group of adolescent adoptees suffered from deficits in self-esteem, impulse control, or sociability, as Simmons had found.

Nonadopted subjects tended to score more positively on the Offer social self dimension ($F = 2.04; p = .15$). A separate analysis of the two

TABLE 2
Intercorrelations of Dependent Ego Identity Measures for All Subjects (N = 91)

	Tan	Interview Family	Interview Peer	School	Self-Esteem	Total	Offer Psychological	OSIQ Social	OSIQ Sexual	OSIQ Family	OSIQ Coping	OSIQ Overall
Tan Ego Identity Scale	—		.24**		.35***	.29**	.36***	.32***	.22*	.19*	.36***	.31**
Interview												
Total Score						—	.40***	.48***		.59***		.57***
Family Factor		—		.31**	.27**	.80***	.24*	.31**		.70***	.24**	.48***
Peer Factor			—		.42***	.54***	.33***	.40***	.32**			.30**
School Factor				—		.54***						.29**
Self-Esteem Factor					—	.60***	.44***	.36***	.26**	.26**	.41***	.31**
Offer Self-Image Questionnaire												
Overall Average Self Score												—
Psychological Self Score							—	.68***	.40***	.46***	.52***	.79***
Social Self Score								—	.44***	.58***	.70***	.88***
Sexual Self Score									—		.24**	.37***
Family Self Score										—	.51***	.80***
Coping Self Score											—	.82***

* p ≤ .05
** p ≤ .01
*** p ≤ .001

TABLE 3
Significant Differences on Ego Identity Measures
for Adopted and Nonadopted Subjects ($N = 91$)

Dependent Measure*	Adopted (N = 50) Mean	Nonadopted (N = 41) Mean	df	F	p
Tan Ego Identity Scale	8.22 (1.67)	7.54 (1.54)	1	4.05	.05
Interview Total Score	72.00 (6.42)	73.05 (7.12)	1	.54	ns
Family Factor	27.26 (3.91)	28.02 (3.73)	1	.89	ns
Peer Factor	21.78 (2.29)	21.56 (2.26)	1	.20	ns
School Factor	9.08 (2.22)	9.61 (2.41)	1	1.18	ns
Self-Esteem Factor	13.88 (1.71)	13.85 (2.11)	1	.004	ns
Offer Self-Image Questionnaire (OSIQ)					
Overall Average Self Score	51.34 (11.41)	53.63 (9.97)	1	1.01	ns
Psychological Self Score	53.02 (12.25)	51.54 (13.05)	1	.31	ns
Social Self Score	50.09 (13.09)	53.81 (11.33)	1	2.04	.15
Sexual Self Score	45.81 (16.58)	47.82 (12.69)	1	.40	ns
Family Self Score	50.38 (14.15)	53.36 (14.66)	1	.96	ns
Coping Self Score	52.38 (13.69)	55.78 (11.06)	1	1.64	ns

*All scores except for OSIQ are reported as raw scores. Scores on the OSIQ have been converted to scale scores with a mean score of 50 and a standard deviation of 15.

subscales constituting this dimension (social relationships and vocational and educational goals) reveals that adoptees do somewhat more poorly in the area of vocational and educational goals. As a lower score here is indicative of less effective functioning within the adolescent's academic environment (Offer et al. 1981), one might conclude that adoptees demonstrate more difficulty in this dimension than nonadoptees according to the OSIQ. This finding is reminiscent of Nospitz's (1979) note that the preponderance of children available for adoption tends to fall within the average range of intellectual functioning, perhaps reflecting a slightly skewed population as compared to biological subjects. Although other

TABLE 4
Perceived Effect* of Adoptive Status on Different Spheres in the
Adolescent's Life ($N = 50$)

Type of Effect	Family	Peer	Social	Self-Esteem	Academic
Some effect					
%	2.0	6.0	2.0	12.0**	0
N	(1)	(3)	(1)	(6)	(0)
No effect					
%	98.0	94.0	98.0	88.0	100
N	(49)	(47)	(49)	(44)	(50)
Total					
%	100%	100%	100%	100%	100%
N	(50)	(50)	(50)	(50)	(50)

*Effect has a single directionality (negative), except for the dimension of self-esteem (see below).
**Three of the 6 Ss reported a *positive* effect here.

studies have rejected the notion of an intellectual differential between the two groups (Hoopes et al. 1970; Witmer et al. 1963), more recent findings by Bohman (1972) and Hoopes (1982) have pointed to a greater incidence of school adjustment problems of a behavioral nature in adoptees that perhaps affects academic functioning in the high school years.

In summary, significant differences between the two groups were not found on overall measures of identity and adjustment. In fact, on the Tan Ego Identity Scale, adoptees' scores were significantly higher at the .05 level.

When adolescent adoptees were asked specifically how their adoptive status impinged on different areas of their lives (i.e., family, peer, social [dating], self-esteem, and academic), an overwhelming majority reported no significant effect (table 4). In fact, many of the subjects commented on the seeming "absurdity" of the question, remarking that it was not adoptive status but other factors that tended to account for difficulties in these spheres. With regard to the self-esteem dimension, some adoptees reported that the fact of adoption actually enhanced their feelings of self-worth by creating a feeling of "specialness" because of their "chosen" status.

How can these findings be explained in light of the bulk of adoption literature that furnishes overriding indications to the contrary? It is the authors' contention that the discrepancy can best be understood on the basis of differences in sampling population. Most theoretical assumptions in the literature were made by clinicians who were attempting to account for pathology in their adoptive psychiatric patients. Certainly, the study of pathology as a means of understanding normality will, in all probability, bias pictures of the norm. It was expected that the use of a nonclinical, normative group of adoptees would present a less biased view of their adjustment in adolescence. It appears that the data confirmed this.

Nonetheless, two issues are worth mentioning with regard to the results presented above. First, it is important to note that the findings of the study are based on self-report data of the adolescents themselves. Although clinical case study is generally open to bias, and all too frequently allows extensive free rein for subjective impressions, the same argument could be made about the adolescents' phenomenological accounts of their own adjustment. Mischel (1972) and Offer and associates (1981), however, have countered criticisms of this nature with systematically controlled validity studies that have demonstrated the potency of self-ratings. On a more qualitative level, both Offer and associates (1981) and Douvan and Adelson (1966) have characterized the adolescents they interviewed in their surveys as generally open and candid in their remarks. Though there was no method of assessing the validity of the self-report data in the current study, the interviewer's impressions were consistent with the observations noted above. The adolescents interviewed appeared remarkably honest and straightforward, on the whole, lending further support to the interview method as an empirical tool.

The second issue regards the sampling bias of the present study. As both adopted and nonadopted subjects constituted a self-selected group of volunteers, little can be said about the adopted and nonadopted adolescents who chose not to participate. Certainly, volunteers are likely to differ in unspecified personality dimensions from nonvolunteers, thus suggesting caution in generalizing the data to a more random population of subjects.

What Family Variables Affect Identity Formation?

Style of Communication About Adoption

It was hypothesized that adopted subjects who perceived an open communication style about adoption within their family would obtain higher scores on measures of ego identity than subjects from families in which the issue of adoption was perceived to be closed. A comparison of identity scores for all adopted subjects along this specific variable is reported in table 5. Style of communication about adoption was determined by subjects' responses to an item (question 9) on the Interview measure that distinguished the presence of adoption discussion from the lack thereof. An inspection of the means for both groups indicates that where significant differences were obtained, they were in the predicted direction. More specifically, open styles of communication about adoption were found to produce significantly higher identity scores among adoptees on the Interview total score, as well as school and self-esteem subfactors ($F = 5.59; p \leq .05; F = 7.24; p < .05 > .01$;

TABLE 5

The Effect of Open vs. Closed Communication Style on Identity Formation of Adopted Adolescents ($N = 50$)

Dependent Measure*	Open Style	Closed Style	df	F	p
Tan Ego Identity Score	8.50	7.86	1	1.82	.18
	(1.55)	(1.78)			
Interview Total Score	73.82	69.68	1	5.59	.02
	(6.31)	(5.90)			
Family Factor	27.57	26.86	1	.39	ns
	(3.72)	(4.20)			
Peer Factor	22.17	21.27	1	1.95	.16
	(2.29)	(2.25)			
School Factor	9.78	8.18	1	7.24	.009
	(2.20)	(1.94)			
Self Esteem Factor	14.28	13.36	1	3.78	.06
	(1.90)	(1.29)			
Offer Self-Image Questionnaire (OSIQ)					
Overall Average Self Score	51.75	50.80	1	.08	ns
	(14.13)	(6.83)			
Psychological Self Score	52.98	53.07	1	.001	ns
	(14.88)	(8.11)			
Social Self Score	50.22	49.93	1	.006	ns
	(15.49)	(9.56)			
Sexual Self Score	44.20	47.87	1	.59	ns
	(16.57)	(16.75)			
Family Self Score	50.47	50.26	1	.003	ns
	(16.00)	(11.74)			
Coping Self Score	53.28	51.23	1	.27	ns
	(17.18)	(7.46)			

*All scores except for OSIQ are reported as raw scores. Scores on the OSIQ have been converted to scale scores with a mean scale score of 50 and a standard deviation of 15.

$F = 3.78$; $p < .10$). A trend in the hypothesized direction was also noted on the Interview peer dimension. Although significant differences in performance on the Tan Ego Identity Scale and OSIQ were not obtained for the different styles, a trend was again noted in the hypothesized direction, with open styles yielding somewhat higher scores.

The predictive strength of the variable under consideration might have been diminished by the fact that all the adopted subjects in the current study had been exposed from birth to at least a minimum of ongoing discussion about adoption, based on their participation in the Delaware Family Study. Style of communication about adoption might be more predictive of identity outcome in a random sample of adoptees who have not participated in a longitudinal adoption study. The current findings nevertheless tend to provide empirical evidence for the theoretical ideas of Blum (1976), Schoenberg (1974), and Sorosky and associates (1977), who strongly advocate a climate of openness in discussions of adoptive status. One would have to agree, based on the present findings, that families who encourage open discussion of the facts tend to produce more secure, identity-solid adolescents. Adoption practitioners would be wise to stress the importance of communication style from the outset, as an open style over time clearly seems to be a predictive factor for positive identity outcome in adolescence.

Quality of Family Relationships

It was thought that adoptees manifesting qualitatively good relationships with their adoptive parents would obtain higher scores on measures of identity than adoptees whose parental relationships were less than satisfying.

Table 6 contains the mean scores on the Tan Ego Identity Scale and the Offer (Overall Average Self Score) for adolescents (adopted and non-adopted) reporting satisfactory and less than satisfactory parental relationships. Quality of relationship was determined by a median split on the family factor scores from the Interview measure. For the most part, highly significant differences between groups reporting satisfactory and unsatisfactory family relationships were noted. On the OSIQ Overall Average Self Score, for example, quality of relationship accounted for differences in the adopted group ($F = 13.80$; $p \leq .001$) and in the nonadopted group ($F = 12.90$; $p = .001$). Although significant differences in Tan Ego Identity scores were obtained for this family variable in nonadopted subjects ($F = 7.87$; $p \leq .008$), only slight differences on this scale were evidenced in the adopted group, suggesting the presence of a measurement artifact that needs to be teased apart by other measures. All in all, results seemed to indicate that good parental relationships promote healthy adjustment in all subjects, thus corroborating the predictive strength of this variable for the adopted adolescent.

Offer and associates (1981, 65) have stated that "if everything else is kept constant, the family will contribute relatively more to the positive development of adolescents than any other psychosocial variable." Obviously, the contribution of positive family ties to overall adjustment is not a novel idea. Adoption theorists (Barinbaum 1974; Glatzer 1955; Goodman and Magno-Nora 1975; McWhinnie 1969, Rickarby and Egan 1980) have recognized the impact of good parental relationships on successful identity outcome in adolescence. However, what appears lacking in the theoretical literature on the specific identity problems in the adoptee is an emphasis on the preventive effect of positive relationships on identity problems in this group. Based on the empirical results obtained thus far, one might conclude

TABLE 6

A Comparison of Mean Scores on Two Measures of Identity Formation for Adolescents Reporting Satisfactory and Unsatisfactory Family Relationships* for All Subjects (N = 91)

Dependent Measure**	Adopted Ss (N = 50)					Nonadopted Ss (N = 41)				
	Satisfactory	Unsatisfactory	df	F	p	Satisfactory	Unsatisfactory	df	F	p
Tan Ego Identity Scale	8.44	8.00	1	.86	ns	8.14	6.90	1	7.87	.008
	(1.55)	(1.77)				(1.62)	(1.17)			
Offer Overall Average Self Score (OSIQ)	56.68	45.99	1	13.80	.001	59.31	47.67	1	20.90	.000
	(7.81)	(12.07)				(8.96)	(7.19)			

*Satisfactory and unsatisfactory assignment based on median split of family factor scores from interview.

**All scores except for OSIQ are reported as raw scores. Scores on the OSIQ have been converted to scale scores with a mean scale score of 50 and a standard deviation of 15.

that satisfactory family relationships could perhaps effectively mitigate or even eliminate the "intensification" of identity concerns that many (e.g., Frisk 1964; Schoenberg 1974) attribute to the inherent stresses of the adoptive situation. Although the intricacies that adoptive status brings to the formation of identity cannot be denied, there appears to be no empirical evidence that links the existence of problems to the fact of adoption, per se. Rather, the data seem to suggest that what promotes healthy identity formation in all adolescents is the quality of family relationships.

Effect of Family Composition on Identity

It was predicted that the presence of nonadopted siblings in the adoptive family would impede the overall adjustment of the adolescent adoptee, as revealed in lower scores when compared to both nonadopted subjects and adopted subjects without a mixed family composition (i.e., having no nonadopted siblings).

The present findings showed no significant differences in the predicted direction when mixed subjects were compared with nonmixed and nonadopted adolescents. In fact, the mixed group obtained slightly higher scores on several of the self-dimensions of the OSIQ. Caution, however, must be maintained in interpreting these results, as the sample size of the mixed group was quite small ($n = 11$).

Empirical literature concerning the impact of this variable on overall adjustment has consistently emphasized the stresses that mixed family composition imposes on adoptive individuals (Hoopes 1982; McWhinnie 1967). How, then, can the present findings be explained? For one, it is important to bear in mind the difficulty in generalizing from results obtained on a sample of 11. Certainly, the likelihood exists that results more consistent with the literature might have been obtained were the groups of comparable size. However, significant differences between mixed and nonmixed groups were noted by Hoopes (1982) on a comparable sample size and population of subjects (the Delaware Family Study Longitudinal Research Project)—in fact, the same population of subjects, only at a younger age, from which the current sample was drawn. One explanation for this divergence might be that adolescence, with all its concomitant consolidations and stresses, acts as an equalizer between groups. Perhaps adolescence does afford subjects a "second individuation," that is, a second chance at personality integration, an observation that Blos (1967) has advanced, thus wiping out differences that might have appeared in earlier stages of development.

Qualitatively, it might be important to note that the mixed subjects impressed the authors quite favorably. There was no gross clinical evidence of greater adjustment difficulty in this group. In fact, according to the subjects' own reports, the presence of nonadopted siblings was viewed as an advantage, that is, as confirmation of their own self-worth enhanced by the realization of their egalitarian treatment within the family. Perhaps, then, when self-reflection becomes a significant part of their makeup, these "mixed" adolescent subjects can benefit from the added recognition that adoptive status does not diminish their esteem within the family.

Does the Degree of Identity Consolidation Affect the Presence of Search Behavior in Adolescent Adoptees?

It was hypothesized that searchers would comprise those adolescents who obtained either very high or extremely low identity scores, that is, evidence of search behavior would be found more pervasively in adolescents who score at the extreme ends on measures of ego identity, thus manifesting either prominent signs of consolidation or marked diffusion. Searchers were defined as those subjects who described themselves as actively seeking information, with or without the intention of meeting their biological parents. Intention was not considered a mandatory attribute because of the legal restrictions on actually pursuing records imposed by the age of the subjects.

Data were analyzed by analysis of variance, and results are found in table 7. An examination of the results reveals that on 10 of the 11 possible identity dimensions considered, adolescent searchers obtained slightly lower mean scores. This finding approached significance on one of the three overall identity scores, the Interview total score ($p = .11$). Although the data showed slight differences in one of the predicted directions, there was no evidence to suggest that searchers reflected superior adjustment, as additionally hypothesized. This was ascertained by examining the distribution of searchers' identity scores, which showed no tendency to cluster at the extreme ends of the scale as had been predicted. In sum, in spite of the lower identity scores found in the search group, a polarized phenomenon could not be confirmed.

Perhaps more noteworthy was the suggestion of less satisfactory family relationships among searchers. Searchers scored significantly lower than non-searchers on the Interview family factor score ($F = 5.15; p < .05$), and their lower scores tended to approach significance on the OSIQ family self score ($p = .12$). Results here seemed to corroborate findings by McWhinnie (1969) and Triseliotis (1973), who have linked search behavior to dissatisfaction with the adoptive parents and with the adoptees themselves, although caution must be used in generalizing from a sample size of 16 in this study. More will be said later about the connection between family relationships and search behavior.

Some theorists have proposed that the presence of search behavior says less about the adoptee's familial relationships and more about the lack of adequate genealogical information available to the adoptee. The question was then asked whether adoptees who manifested search behavior in this sample were more inclined to be dissatisfied with the information given to them about their adoption. Results, however, were not conclusive along this dimension, as a significant relationship was not found between search behavior and dissatisfaction (chi square = .70; $p > .10$).

Regarding the extent of search behavior in this sample, it was found that the majority of adolescents interviewed (68%) revealed no desire to search. Thus, while an interest in genealogical information was expressed by most of the adoptees, only 16 (32%) out of 50 actually wished to pursue information

TABLE 7
A Comparison of Identity Scores for Searchers and Nonsearchers ($N = 50$)

Dependent Measure*	Searchers ($N = 16$)	Nonsearchers ($N = 34$)	df	F	p
Tan Ego Identity Scale	8.69 (1.40)	8.00 (1.76)	1	1.88	ns
Interview Total Score	69.88 (5.57)	73.00 (6.63)	1	2.66	.11
Family Factor	25.50 (3.67)	28.09 (3.80)	1	5.15	.03
Peer Factor	21.56 (2.68)	21.88 (2.13)	1	.21	ns
School Factor	9.00 (2.31)	9.11 (2.21)	1	.03	ns
Self-Esteem Factor	13.81 (1.60)	13.91 (1.78)	1	.04	ns
Offer Self-Image Questionnaire (OSIQ)					
Overall Average Self Score	48.53 (14.92)	52.66 (9.31)	1	1.44	ns
Psychological Self Score	51.01 (15.37)	53.98 (10.62)	1	.63	ns
Social Self Score	49.31 (16.14)	50.47 (11.65)	1	.08	ns
Sexual Self Score	47.69 (16.46)	44.94 (16.81)	1	.30	ns
Family Self Score	45.87 (15.87)	52.51 (12.97)	1	2.47	.12
Coping Self Score	49.78 (18.11)	53.62 (11.16)	1	.85	ns

*All scores except for OSIQ are reported as raw scores. Scores on the OSIQ have been converted to scale scores with a mean scale score of 50 and a standard deviation of 15.

more aggressively, confirming the observation made by the American Academy of Pediatrics (1971) that not all adoptees want to search. Again, it is important to note that the mean age of the sample was 16.6 years, considerably below the age that would permit legal access to birth records. It has been found that the attainment of adult legal status tends to accelerate genealogic concerns (reported in Sorosky et al. 1975). Because of the limited number of 18-year-olds in this study, however, it was difficult to corroborate this finding.

One final point is worth mentioning. Although both clinical and empirical studies (Farber 1977; McWhinnie 1969) have reported a greater prevalence of search behavior among females, no significant sex differences were found in the present study (chi square $= .91; p > .10$), although a slightly larger number of searchers (9 out of 16) were female. Again, the small sample size makes it impossible to draw any sound conclusions with regard to the age and sex differences noted here.

Does Style of Communication About Adoption Affect the Presence of Search Behavior in Adolescent Adoptees?

It was hypothesized that perceived openness in communication would result in decreased search behavior. Findings indicated, however, a nonsignificant relationship between open communication and an interest in searching, despite Clothier's (1943) comments to the contrary. On the basis of these results and the fact that searchers as a group obtained lower family scores on measures of adjustment, it was decided to investigate further the relationship between family factors and search behavior.

When the family relationships of searchers and nonsearchers were compared, some significant differences emerged (table 8). Results showed a far greater number of searchers (75%) reporting unsatisfactory family relationships in contrast to nonsearchers, who seemed significantly more satis-

TABLE 8
Perceived Quality of Family Relationships and Search Behavior
in the Adoptee ($N = 50$)

Search Behavior	Satisfactory	Quality of Relationship Unsatisfactory	Total
Searchers	25.0	75.0	100.0
Nonsearchers	61.8	38.2	100.0

chi square $= 4.50$
$df = 1 \ p < .05$

fied with the quality of their family ties (chi square $= 4.5$, $p < .05$), again demonstrating the predictive strength of this family variable. Data thus seem to indicate that positive family relationships do, in fact, reduce the need to search in this age group, once more confirming Triseliotis's (1973) formulations on search behavior and its relationship to ungratifying family ties.

Does Family Composition Affect the Presence of Search Behavior in Adolescent Adoptees?

It was predicted that adoptees from families with nonadopted siblings would be more inclined to search because of the possible stress imposed by their family composition. Examination of the data revealed nonsignificant findings along this dimension (chi square $= .51$; $p > .10$). One may conclude, then, that genealogical concerns (as manifested in search behavior) were not enhanced by the presence of nonadopted siblings. This finding, however, is consistent with previous findings that mixed family composition was not predictive of adjustment difficulties in this sample of adoptees. Further research on a larger scale would have to be done before generalizing these results to "mixed" adoptees as a whole.

SUMMARY

In summary, adopted subjects were not found to have greater difficulties along the dimension of identity formation than nonadopted subjects, that is, adoptive status in and of itself was not predictive of greater stress among adolescents in this study. The impact of selected family variables on identity in the adoptee revealed that quality of family relationships was most predictive of positive identity outcome across all groups. Perceived style of communication about adoption issues was found to have some impact on adjustment, though results were not highly significant. The significance of family composition as a variable in identity outcome was not confirmed.

Finally, an investigation of search behavior in the adolescent adoptee was conducted. It was found that searchers as a group performed somewhat more poorly across identity measures than nonsearchers, with a significantly poorer showing in the area of family relationships. Further exploration of two specific family variables selected for study revealed no significant findings. Neither style of communication about adoption nor family composition as defined by the presence of nonadopted siblings was found to be predictive of search behavior in this group of adoptees. Perceived quality of family relationships, however, did show significant predictive strength as a variable, corroborating theoretical notions that unsatisfactory family ties can, in fact, heighten an adolescent's desire to search.

ADDITIONAL FINDINGS

Sex Differences

The literature indicates the existence of sex differences in level of identity formation, with females frequently scoring higher than males on various measures of identity (Josselson et al. 1977b; Start and Traxler 1974). This variable was explored in the present research.

Table 9 contains a comparison of mean identity scores for all male and female subjects. An inspection of the data shows that on all the overall identity measures, female adolescents scored significantly higher than males,

TABLE 9
A Comparison of Mean Scores on Identity Measures for Male and Female Subjects ($N = 91$)

Dependent Measure*	Males (N = 44)	Females (N = 47)	df	F	p
Tan Ego Identity Scale	7.61 (1.63)	8.19 (1.61)	1	2.89	.09
Interview Total Score	70.43 (7.08)	74.38 (5.83)	1	8.49	.005
Family Factor	26.84 (3.87)	28.32 (3.69)	1	3.48	.07
Peer Factor	21.16 (2.40)	22.17 (2.05)	1	4.69	.03
School Factor	8.73 (2.59)	9.87 (1.87)	1	5.89	.02
Self-Esteem Factor	13.71 (2.06)	14.02 (1.73)	1	.63	ns
Offer Self-Image Questionnaire (OSIQ)					
Overall Average Self Score	48.61 (11.72)	55.90 (8.55)	1	11.62	.001
Psychological Self Score	49.14 (13.55)	55.36 (10.88)	1	5.87	.02
Social Self Score	47.48 (13.20)	55.78 (10.19)	1	11.35	.001
Sexual Self Score	45.29 (17.30)	48.06 (12.31)	1	.78	ns
Family Self Score	47.78 (15.81)	55.42 (11.92)	1	6.82	.01
Coping Self Score	49.96 (13.45)	57.62 (10.67)	1	9.10	.003

*All scores except for OSIQ are reported as raw scores. Scores on the OSIQ have been converted to scale scores with a mean scale score of 50 and a standard deviation of 15.

thus providing additional support for the findings of Josselson and associates (1977b), whose results were also based on a normative high school population. The lack of significant sex differences in the self-esteem subfactor of the Interview measure coincided with Offer's (1981) findings of no difference in overall self-esteem scores on the OSIQ. However, Offer's reported trend for males to score slightly higher across most OSIQ self-dimensions was not confirmed by the present data. Though there were no significant sex differences in the sexual self score among adolescents in this study, the remainder of subfactor scores across measures showed significantly higher perfor-

TABLE 10
Sex Differences in Identity Scores for Adopted and Nonadopted Subjects ($N = 91$)

Dependent Measure*	Adopted ($N = 50$)		Non-Adopted ($N = 41$)		df	F	p
	Male ($N = 24$)	Female ($N = 26$)	Male ($N = 20$)	Female ($N = 21$)			
Tan Ego Identity Scale	7.88 (1.68)	8.54 (1.63)	7.30 (1.56)	7.76 (1.51)	3	2.37	.08
Interview Total Score	70.71 (6.04)	73.19 (6.65)	70.10 (8.32)	75.86 (4.32)	3	3.54	.02
Family Factor	27.38 (3.37)	27.15 (4.42)	26.20 (4.40)	29.76 (1.70)	3	3.55	.02
Peer Factor	20.88 (2.53)	22.62 (1.72)	21.50 (2.26)	21.62 (2.31)	3	2.67	.05
School Factor	8.54 (2.25)	9.58 (2.12)	8.95 (3.00)	10.24 (1.48)	3	2.40	.07
Self-Esteem Factor	13.92 (1.82)	13.85 (1.64)	13.45 (2.35)	14.24 (1.84)	3	.59	ns
Offer Self-Image Questionnaire (OSIQ)							
Overall Average Self Score	47.51 (12.96)	54.87 (8.60)	49.91 (10.22)	57.18 (8.52)	3	4.23	.01
Psychological Self Score	49.74 (13.73)	56.06 (10.05)	48.43 (13.64)	54.50 (12.03)	3	2.02	.12
Social Self Score	44.62 (14.42)	55.15 (9.46)	50.91 (10.97)	56.57 (11.23)	3	4.96	.003
Sexual Self Score	43.03 (20.06)	48.39 (12.44)	48.00 (13.28)	47.65 (12.44)	3	.67	ns
Family Self Score	46.92 (14.51)	53.58 (13.29)	48.81 (17.57)	57.69 (9.80)	3	2.65	.05
Coping Self Score	48.70 (16.37)	55.79 (9.80)	51.49 (8.97)	59.88 (11.50)	3	3.67	.02

*All scores except for OSIQ are reported as raw scores. Scores on the OSIQ have been converted to scale scores with a mean scale score of 50 and a standard deviation of 15.

mance for females. The overwhelmingly positive picture of feminine identity development demonstrated here is difficult to account for theoretically. It is possible that adolescent females within this age range are somewhat more developmentally advanced in identity formation, although more research would have to substantiate this.

Perhaps more pertinent to this specific study is the impact of adoptive status on the variable of sex. Sex differences in identity scores for adopted and nonadopted subjects are reported in table 10. For the most part, female adopted subjects scored higher than male adopted adolescents and significantly so on the Interview peer factor (Student-Newman-Kuels a posteriori test [$p < .05$]). A similar trend was noted in nonadopted subjects, with females showing significantly better performance than males on the Interview total score ($p < .05$) and the Interview family factor score ($p < .05$).

An examination of the data on the OSIQ corroborated this trend. Again, female adoptees scored significantly higher than male adoptees on the overall average self score, the social self and coping self dimensions (as confirmed by a posteriori tests, $p < .05$). Nonadopted females evidenced superior performance when compared to both adopted and nonadopted male adolescents. This discrepancy between male and female nonadoptees reached significance on the coping self dimension and the overall average self score (again as confirmed by a posteriori tests [$p < .05$]). Thus, female nonadoptees as a group compared most favorably to all other groups, and male adoptees as a rule scored most poorly, though not significantly lower than nonadopted males.

In sum, although the adoption literature does not address the issue of sex differences in identity formation, the present findings indicate that female adoptees in this study were somewhat better adjusted than their male counterparts. Moreover, the results indicate that adoptive status does not significantly alter the general trend of sex differences in identity scores.

Age Differences

On the basis of the fact that identity formation was found to be a positively increasing function of age in almost all previous studies on college populations (Constantinople 1969; Dignan 1965; Marcia 1980; Stark and Traxler 1974), age differences were examined in the present study. An examination of differences in identity scores for all subjects across age, however, proved to be nonsignificant.

Initially, it was thought that the limited number of subjects within each age level studied accounted for the lack of significant age findings in the present study. However, Offer and associates' (1981) similar findings on a sample size of approximately 15,000 subjects ruled out this possibility. Perhaps what can be concluded is that sizable increments in identity formation do not occur within the high school years, but manifest themselves over a much lengthier period of time as Marcia (1980) has suggested in his writings on identity.

Significant Social Atom Findings

As mentioned in chapter 3, the Social Atom task was selected as an additional and less structured means of assessing some of the relationship data gleaned from the other three self-report measures. The rationale for its inclusion was to provide some consensual validation across measures, thereby enhancing the validity and reliability of the data obtained through more direct means. In addition, the lack of sociometric norms for either the modal adolescent or the adolescent adoptee promoted an interest in determining whether the profiles for these two groups might differ.

It was thought that adolescents with an extremely limited social network would be less well adjusted than those with a more expansive or varied network of significant others. The data show that the number of category types (mother, father, same sex peers, opposite sex peers, relatives and non-family adults) did correlate with the Tan Ego Identity Scale ($r = .32, p < .01$) and the Interview total score ($r = .30$, $p < .01$). Likewise the total number of people in the Social Atom correlated with the Offer Social Self Score ($r = .26$, $p < .01$), the Coping Self Score ($r = .34, p < .001$), and Average Self Score ($r = .26$, $p < .01$). These findings are in line with data reported by Josselson and associates (1977) on high maturity adolescents, who revealed a highly complex and differentiated object world.

Adolescents who totally omit either peers or parents from their Social Atom or whose influence scores for either group is zero, were assumed to be less adapted than those adolescents who designated influential representatives from both peers and parent groups. Data here indicated that of all the Social Atom variables, the influence of mother, the influence of father, and combined parental influence were most predictive of adjustment, as revealed by the sizable and significant correlation between these variables and the Interview total score. ($r = .51, p < .001; r = .47, p < .001; r = .54, p < .001$, respectively). Significant relationships were similarly found between the same Social Atom variables and the Offer average self score. However, neither the number of peers nor their influence status correlated significantly with any of the overall identity measures. In fact, "number of same sex peers" correlated negatively ($r = -.22, p \leq .05$) with these measures. Although this is a low correlation, it may suggest on the one hand that adolescents who had overloaded their Social Atom with peers were less likely to be among the well adjusted. On the other hand, omission of peers did not necessarily predict poor adjustment, as had been initially assumed.

The Social Atom categorical variables were analyzed next. Table 11 contains data relating the Social Atom "category with the highest influence score" to the dependent measures of identity. Significant results were obtained, demonstrating the predictive strength of the "parent and peer" category for overall adjustment. More specifically, those adolescents who attributed highest influence to both parents and peers in combination scored significantly higher on identity measures than those attributing influence solely to peers or other category types. The significance of this finding was further confirmed by the Student-Newman-Keuls a posteriori test for

TABLE 11

The Relationship Between Category With Highest Influence Score (Social Atom) and Overall Identity ($N = 91$)

Dependent Measure*	Parent Only	Peer Only	Parent and Peer	Other Category/ Combination	df	F	p
Tan Ego Identity Scale	7.89 (1.85)	8.04 (1.59)	8.57 (1.70)	7.44 (1.33)	3	1.53	ns
Interview Total Score	74.96 (5.04)	69.36 (7.15)	76.07 (5.68)	70.88 (6.80)	3	5.55	.002
Family Factor	29.04 (2.26)	25.72 (4.10)	29.21 (4.21)	27.04 (3.90)	3	4.83	.004
Peer Factor	21.11 (2.71)	21.44 (2.24)	22.93 (.92)	21.84 (2.14)	3	2.20	.09
School Factor	10.26 (2.09)	8.36 (2.27)	10.14 (2.11)	8.80 (2.26)	3	4.39	.006
Self-Esteem Factor	14.56 (1.91)	13.84 (1.82)	13.79 (1.53)	13.20 (1.98)	3	2.34	.08
Offer Self-Image Questionnaire (OSIQ)							
Overall Average Self Score	54.21 (13.43)	50.04 (9.56)	58.44 (8.99)	49.32 (8.09)	3	2.97	.04
Psychological Self Score	52.23 (16.00)	54.38 (9.17)	56.80 (9.66)	47.98 (12.04)	3	1.86	.14
Social Self Score	50.57 (14.56)	51.40 (13.49)	58.09 (9.84)	49.88 (9.17)	3	1.52	ns
Sexual Self Score	43.73 (15.36)	47.59 (19.24)	50.24 (13.22)	47.11 (9.77)	3	.65	ns
Family Self Score	56.75 (15.05)	45.42 (11.68)	60.91 (11.01)	47.45 (13.78)	3	6.28	.001
Coping Self Score	57.20 (14.04)	50.12 (14.39)	57.91 (11.16)	51.93 (8.31)	3	2.11	.10

*All scores except for OSIQ are reported as raw scores. Scores on the OSIQ have been converted to scale scores with a mean scale score of 50 and a standard deviation of 15.

(1) the Interview total score, which significantly differentiated "parent and peer" ($p < .05$) from "peer only" and "other category/combination"; (2) the Interview family factor, which was found to significantly differentiate "parent and peer" from "peer only," as well as "parent only" from "peer only"; (3) the Interview school factor, where results paralleled those obtained for the family factor; and (4) the Interview self factor, for which "parent only" differed significantly from "other category combination." While the OSIQ yielded similar results, the only dimension that was found to differentiate significantly between groups according to a posteriori analysis was the family self, in which scores for "parent and peer" combinations and "parent only" were substantially higher than the other two categories.

Similar trends were noted when data were examined that related the Social Atom variable "types closest in proximity to the self" to identity scores (table 12). Again, highest scoring adolescents were those who chose "parent and peer" combinations. This finding reached significance (as confirmed by a posteriori tests) on (1) the Interview total score and the Interview family factor where adolescents selecting "parent and peer" combinations differed significantly from those placing "peers only" closest to themselves. Although the Offer family self dimension was similarly differentiating for adolescents choosing "parent and peer" combinations, a Student-Newman-Kuels analysis revealed no sharply significant differences ($p < .05$).

There was no indication that the presence of *both* same and opposite sex peers in an adolescent's Social Atom predicted better adjustment for this age group. Perhaps Offer and colleagues (1981, 88) are correct in concluding that "the modal adolescent moves slowly in the direction of heterosexuality." At least the present data confirm the lack of correlations noted in the identity literature between identity status and heterosexual behavior in adolescents of high school age (Josselson et al. 1977a, b).

To summarize, results seem to reflect some highly consistent and interesting trends. Perhaps most significant is the fact that high identity adolescents tend to have relational systems that include both parents and peers to whom they attribute closeness and influence. Although the omission of peers from categories of "influence" or "closeness to self" tends to result in slightly lower adjustment scores, the omission is not as significant as might be expected. What tends to be most strongly predictive of maladjustment is the exclusion of parents from either category. More specifically, those adolescents whose Social Atom was composed *solely* of peers or other combinations (relatives, nonfamily adults, etc.) scored most poorly on measures of identity.

What implications can be drawn from these results? It seems safe to conclude that adolescents who function well have parental figures who serve as "anchors" for them, providing both a sense of intimacy and a set of guidelines for appropriate behavior. When these two requisites exist, the

TABLE 12
The Relationship Between Types Closest in Proximity to the
Self (Social Atom) and Overall Identity ($N = 91$)

Dependent Measure*	Parent Only	Peer Only	Parent and Peer	Other Category/ Combination	df	F	p
Tan Ego Identity Scale	8.12 (1.90)	7.83 (1.75)	8.32 (1.53)	7.63 (1.48)	3	.82	ns
Interview Total Score	73.35 (5.18)	69.52 (8.18)	75.58 (5.49)	72.28 (6.30)	3	3.14	.03
Family Factor	28.41 (3.26)	25.61 (4.47)	28.95 (3.39)	27.81 (3.43)	3	3.40	.02
Peer Factor	21.12 (2.69)	21.65 (1.99)	22.32 (1.83)	21.63 (2.46)	3	.85	ns
School Factor	9.65 (2.18)	8.91 (2.43)	10.05 (1.99)	9.00 (2.44)	3	1.20	ns
Self-Esteem Factor	14.18 (1.38)	13.35 (2.33)	14.26 (1.73)	13.84 (1.87)	3	1.01	ns
Offer Self-Image Questionnaire (OSIQ)							
Overall Average Self Score	52.69 (15.51)	50.43 (10.94)	56.93 (8.42)	50.89 (8.37)	3	1.68	.19
Psychological Self Score	50.72 (17.38)	51.31 (13.96)	57.46 (10.28)	50.95 (9.10)	3	1.34	ns
Social Self Score	50.92 (15.21)	51.80 (12.42)	54.83 (10.86)	50.38 (11.88)	3	.54	ns
Sexual Self Score	43.17 (18.20)	43.67 (16.83)	50.41 (12.10)	48.61 (12.76)	3	1.21	ns
Family Self Score	55.18 (19.05)	47.42 (12.26)	58.28 (11.04)	49.08 (13.47)	3	2.86	.04
Coping Self Score	53.91 (15.19)	52.44 (14.12)	57.08 (10.55)	53.10 (11.37)	3	.54	ns

*All scores except for OSIQ are reported as raw scores. Scores on the OSIQ have been converted to scale scores with a mean scale score of 50 and a standard deviation of 15.

process of identity formation seems able to assume a healthy course. These conclusions are consistent with the observations of Offer and associates (1981), Coleman (1978) and Douvan and Adelson (1966), who have disputed the "storm and stress" theory of adolescence that describes this period as one fraught with disturbance and disruption between the generations. As Offer (cited in Coleman 1978) noted:

> Continuity of values can be seen…between the parent generation and the adolescent.…Peer group values do have an influence on behavior, but most often the influence can be negated by the stronger inculcated parental values. This

conflict, however, seems to be minimal as peer group
values themselves are likely to be extensions of parental
values. (p. 4)

Josselson and associates (1977a) similarly found that high maturity
adolescents were close to a parental figure in the family who would approve
of them. They (1977, 51) write: "It is this fundamental, historically important source of self-esteem that allows peer relations to be ancillary and to be
experienced in perspective. The lack of such a relationship...leads to a sense
of inferiority and a hunger for objects which will mitigate that hurt." Perhaps
the adolescents in this study who chose the "other" category in their Social
Atom were those seeking replacements for unsuitable parental objects. Thus,
where parental values and influences are in balance with peers, and where
relationships with one or both parents are felt to be emotionally gratifying,
adjustment is solid—again attesting to the importance of positive family relationships in the overall process of identity consolidation. The fact that this
result emerged from the Social Atom findings further augments the validity
and reliability of the Interview measure.

One final question remains for discussion—whether adopted, nonadopted and mixed adopted and nonadopted adolescents living together
differed significantly in their Social Atom profiles. A chi square analysis was
performed for the two categorical variables, "category with the highest
influence score" and "types closest to the self." For the category "types closest to self," no significant difference was found across groups (chi square =
3.41; df = 6; $p > .10$). For the "highest influence" category, however, some
differences were obtained, although not at an acceptable level of significance
(chi square = 9.14; df = 6; $p < .20 > .10$). Perhaps most noteworthy was the
fact that 17% of the nonadoptive group chose the "peers only" category, in
contrast to 36% of the total adoptive group. Although percentages of
adopted and nonadopted adolescents selecting "parent only" and "parent
and peer" were nearly the same, a slightly higher percentage (36.6%) of the
nonadoptive group selected the "other category/combination," as compared
to adopted subjects (20%). Generally speaking, profiles for adoptive and nonadoptive groups were not dissimilar enough to warrant further analysis.

It might be of interest to note that no adoptees included their biological
parents in their Social Atom, either spontaneously or after the suggestion
was made. This held for both searchers and nonsearchers alike, perhaps
confirming the fact that while an interest in searching for their biological
parents might be compelling for some adoptees, "it is with their adoptive
parents that adopted adolescents primarily identify" (McWhinnie 1969,
135). In sum, although biological parents may exist in the fantasy lives of the
adoptees, they appear to have no place in the adopted adolescent's relational
system.

PHENOMENOLOGICAL ADOPTION DATA

Few research endeavors of this nature have sought to supplement empirical data with qualitative information pertaining to the adoptive experience of normal adolescents. Although adoption theorists have speculated on a multitude of issues germane to identity formation in the adolescent adoptee, their ideas have been limited by the inherent biases of their clinical samples. Because the adolescents of this study were mature enough to reflect on some of the very issues debated in the literature, it was decided to ask them directly for a phenomenological account of selected aspects of their adoptive experience.

Timing of Disclosure

As mentioned in an earlier discussion of the identity process in adoptees, the issue of disclosure has received considerable attention from theorists and clinicians alike. Although current adoption practice advocates early disclosure (American Academy of Pediatrics Committee on Adoption 1971), others have been adamant about postponing disclosure because of the possibility of deleterious emotional effects of telling a child prior to the resolution of the oedipal complex (Schecter 1960; Wieder 1978). When adopted adolescents in this study were asked for their opinions on disclosure, 92% revealed that the age of disclosure had been satisfactory to them (table 13). It is interesting to note that 92% of the adoptees had reportedly been told by the age of 6, with the largest percentage reporting disclosure between 3 and 5 years of age (table 14). All four subjects who had been told after 6 years were males, who expressed dissatisfaction with the timing of disclosure—two desiring earlier disclosure, one later, and one "not at all" (table 13). It is apparent from the data that the majority of adolescent adoptees studied perceived no deleterious effects from having been told of their adoption early in life, quite contrary to the evidence furnished by clinicians.

TABLE 13
Desired Age of Disclosure About Adoptive Status ($N = 50$)

Age Desired	Percent and Frequency
Earlier	4.0% (2)
Same Age	92.0 (46)
Later	2.0 (1)
Not at all	2.0 (1)
Total	100.0%

TABLE 14
Reported Age of Disclosure About Adoptive Status (*N* = 50)

Years	Percent and Frequency	Cumulative Frequency
1	12.0% (6)	12.0
2	14.0 (7)	26.0
3	22.0 (11)	48.0
4	16.0 (8)	64.0
5	18.0 (9)	82.0
6	10.0 (5)	92.0
8	4.0 (2)	96.0
9	2.0 (1)	98.0
12	2.0 (1)	100.0
Total	100.0%	

Mean = 3.94
Mode = 3.00
Median = 3.63
Range = 11

Perhaps of equal significance were the subjects' opinions about when disclosure ought to occur. Results from the entire sample of 91 subjects (adopted and nonadopted) showed that over half the group felt that disclosure should occur before the age of 6, with the explanation that children ought to be told in their formative years, when they are first acquiring knowledge about their world (table 15). When adoptees' opinions were compared to those of nonadoptees, however, some interesting and significant differences surfaced (table 16). For example, 74% of adoptees believed that disclosure should occur before the age of 6, as compared to only 34.1% of nonadoptees ($p < .001$). Even more significant is the fact that 24.4% of nonadoptees but only 2% of adoptees suggested disclosure after the age of 12. One might anticipate that those who had personally experienced early disclosure as a positive phenomenon would tend to advocate for it, as com-

TABLE 15
Adolescents' Opinions About Disclosure — All Subjects (*N* = 91)

Age	Percent and Frequency	
Before 6 Years	56.0%	(51)
6–12 Years	31.9	(29)
Teenage Years	6.6	(6)
Early Adult Years	4.4	(4)
Never	1.1	(1)
Total	100.0%	*N* = 91

TABLE 16
Adopted and Nonadopted Subjects' Opinions About Disclosure ($N = 91$)

Age	Adopted ($N = 50$) Percent and Frequency		Nonadopted ($N = 41$) Percent and Frequency	
Before 6 Years	74.0%	(37)	34.1%	(14)
6–12 Years	24.0	(12)	41.5	(17)
Teenage Years	2.0	(1)	12.2	(5)
Early Adult Years	0	(0)	9.8	(4)
Never	0	(0)	2.4	(1)
Total	100.0%	50	100.0%	41

$df = 4$
chi square $= 18.19$
$p < .001$

pared to nonadopted adolescents, whose lack of familiarity would compel them to rely upon a more intellectual sense of what might be appropriate.

On Searching for Biological Parents

As emphasized earlier, few adolescent adoptees interviewed (16 out of 50) actually wished to search for their biological parents, although all 50 adoptees studied expressed an interest in general background information, with health history heading the list. These findings are somewhat consistent with those of McWhinnie (1969), whose adolescent subjects indicated some curiosity about their biological parents' age, occupation, personality traits, and reasons for placement. What do adolescents actually say about searching for biological parents? Among the pro-search group, reasons for searching seemed to reflect general curiosity, curiosity about adoptive placement, and most of all an unmet need for some form of parental identification or genetic "continuity" (Erikson 1950) that appeared hypertrophied in these particular adolescents. As one 17-year-old girl stated:

> I'd want to know what she looks like, where she's from, and why she gave me up for adoption...to see if she looks anything like me...If she did, it would be weird, but I'd be hoping that she looked like me.

And another 17-year-old reflected:

> I only want to see if I look like my natural parents...if I did then I'd want to see if I was like them in any other way. If it was good, I'd like it because then I'd hope to be like that when I got older. I'd also like to see if my interests matched theirs, to see if they were hereditary or environmental. I wonder how tall they were...I'd want to see their kids to see if they would look like I did.

Interestingly enough, most of the curiosity tended to be directed toward the biological mother regardless of the sex of the adolescent adoptee. Perhaps most emphatic of all the adolescent searchers was a 17½-year-old who commented:

> I want to find out who they are. I'd like to meet them if they are willing to meet me...to find out the reason why they placed me. You should know something about your "natural mother." It's just finding them that I'm concerned about. No matter what they're like, they're still your parents.

A slightly younger, more ambivalent searcher, who seemed unable to take a definitive stance on the issue of searching, tended to romanticize his biological parents in a manner reminiscent of a latency-age child. He said: "I'd like to know who they are in case it's someone like a movie star."

In contrast, nonsearchers as a group seemed to be less intensely curious and more cognizant of their biological parents' rights to a separate and private existence. Said one 17-year-old:

> I've wondered but wouldn't search. They've gone on with their lives now and we wouldn't know how to work each other into our lives.

Similarly, another 17½-year-old female adolescent noted: "I'd be curious about my birthparents, but know it's not right...I wouldn't want to ruin that life...." However, as Frisk (1964) has mentioned, some adolescents express the fear of not being able to integrate genealogical information intrapsychically, in spite of their curiosity. In line with Frisk's remarks is one 15½-year-old's comment: "I've had questions but wouldn't want to find out about my birthparents...I'd have an identity crisis or something."

Because of the many references made by searchers to issues of resemblance between themselves and their biological parents, the question was asked whether searchers as a group perceived themselves as more strikingly mismatched physically within their adoptive families than nonsearchers did. Table 17 provides these results: Substantially more searchers (43.8%) than nonsearchers (17.6%) report a perceived physical dissimilarity to their adoptive parents (chi square $= 2.62, p > .10 < .20$), suggesting that mismatch concerns account for some of the need to search in the developmental period of adolescence when issues of physical appearance are of paramount concern. As searchers in this study exhibited somewhat lower adjustment scores than nonsearchers, perhaps issues of mismatch do, in fact, promote identity concerns that accelerate search behavior in some adoptees.

Fantasies and Feelings About Being Adopted

Related to the issue of early disclosure are the "traumatic sequelae" that Wieder (1977a, b; 1978) presents in his descriptions of the fantasy lives of his patients. Regarding the fact of placement itself, Wieder (1977a, 197) notes that "all three [of his analysands] came to believe that they were literally cast out into the world as helpless infants and had survived independently for a while." Nospitz (1979, 342) similarly reports that "among the frequently experienced fantasies [of the adoptee] are the ideas that he was bad and thus given away, that the biological parents were bad and thus gave him away, or that the adoptive parents kidnapped him." Though Nospitz's comments refer to the fantasy life of a much younger child, both his and Wieder's typify the fantasies generally attributed to adoptees as a group.

When adoptees in this study were asked for their thoughts about why they were placed for adoption, an overwhelming majority (92%) gave realistic reasons for placement. Among the ideas most frequently cited were (1) financial difficulties, (2) emotional immaturity of the biological parents, (3) pregnancy out of wedlock and the illegality of abortions, (4) altruistic reasons, that is, to give the adoptee a better life within a more stable family, and (5) the possibility that the biological parents had not wanted children and simply made a mistake. Only 4 of the 50 adoptees entertained more egocentric ideas referent to the possibility of their own inferiority. These findings seem quite different from those reported by Wieder (1977a, b; 1978), suggesting the degree of bias that results when generalizations are based on clinical samples of adoptees.

The disparity in findings becomes even more marked when adoptees' fantasies of their biological parents are reviewed. Wieder (1977a) recalls that his patients' fantasies

> were not fantasies of idealized or exalted images unsullied by misdeeds. Rather [they were] images of debased and feared people for whom [they] had an unrelieved hatred. (p. 189)

TABLE 17
The Effect of Physical Dissimilarity to the Adoptive Parents on the Need to Search (N = 50)

Search Behavior	Physical Appearance Dissimilar Percent and Frequency	Similar Percent and Frequency	Total Percent and Frequency
Searchers	43.8% (7)	56.2% (9)	100.0% N = 16
Nonsearchers	17.6% (6)	82.4% (28)	100.0% N = 34
	N = 13	N = 37	N = 50

df = 1
chi square = 2.62
p > .10 < .20

Furthermore, he notes that biological parents were typically represented "as corrupt, immoral, sadistic, lower class and uneducated" (Wieder 1977a, 197), quoting one 17-year-old patient who remarked, "I only see my father as a killer and my mother as a whore" (p. 191). Only later does Wieder reveal that this adolescent's adoptive family was characterized by violence and lack of affection.

In sharp contrast, none of the adolescent adoptees in this study who was able to fantasize about his or her biological parents (70%) made disparaging remarks. What was noted was a tendency to project a sameness onto the biological parent in either personality or appearance, perhaps reflecting the need for continuity of character and identification that Erikson (1950) attributes to the adolescent's process of identity formation. For example, one 17-year-old boy said: "My parents [biological parents] would be tall (I'm a lot taller than most)...I think my dad would work a lot because that's all I ever do." Similarly, an 18-year-old boy had this to say:

Dad probably was big...I'm sure he played football...Mom would be kind...They'd be nice people, fun loving...Of course, these thoughts come from me...I'm like that.

Another adolescent boy with a reportedly unhappy home life appeared to be looking for more satisfactory role models with which to identify. He remarked:

They'd be outgoing like me...Pretty reasonable and fair with regard to decisions...pretty athletic, liking to be on the go a lot...I think and act differently from my [adoptive] parents now, so I attribute this to my natural parents.

Thus, even in the case of an ungratifying adoptive relationship, the resultant fantasies still differ dramatically from those cited in the literature. Although one could argue that more constraints exist in a research interview than in an analytic session, it is difficult to dismiss the qualitative discrepancy between the two sets of fantasies, especially when far-reaching generalizations about early disclosure are made on the basis of the expressions of a few analysands.

Little has been written on how it actually feels to be adopted, although what has been documented in the literature is generally negatively tinged. Wieder (1978, 804), for example, notes that many adoptees "don't feel like real people," while Pannor and Nerlove (1977) comment on the strong feelings of rejection that remain a source of ill-feeling in many adoptees. When adolescents in this study were asked to reflect, most seemed to indicate that being adopted produced no ill effects, claiming that it wasn't that much different from being "natural born" as far as they could tell. While two adolescents admitted feeling "second-rate," or "lacking in identity," several mentioned a heightened sense of acceptance and love that their adoptive status occasioned. As one 17-year-old female said: "It makes you feel *wanted* and that's a big part of how you feel."

When all subjects were asked whether adoptees had "a tougher time of it than nonadoptees," most adolescents asserted that it was not adoptive status per se that necessarily engendered difficulty, but problematic relationships within the family, especially with one's parents. However, when adoptees and nonadoptees were asked to fantasize a change in their birth status (from adopted to nonadopted or vice versa), some significant differences were found in their perceptions ($p > .05 < .10$). Although most subjects noted that changes in birth status would not result in a qualitative diminution of their lives, more nonadopted subjects, when viewing a change to adoptive status, felt that a change in status would be problematical. Perhaps Nospitz (1979) is correct in his assumption that society tends to be disparaging of adoptive status. Reflecting on the attitude of the general public toward adoption, one 15½-year-old boy poignantly stated:

> It's not adoption that is the problem but what other people
> think of adopted kids. They're always shown in movies as
> "the druggie."

In sum, how do adolescents feel about being adopted? Blum (1976) quotes from the reflections of a female adoptee who also happens to be an adoptive parent:

> Adopted children feel *curious*, that's how they feel; they
> may also feel happy, sad, buoyant, anxious, competent,
> depressed, not because they are adopted, but because they
> are individual children, growing up in particular families.
> That's the point that the courts, the experts, and the
> authors seem to miss: once you accept the curiosity as a
> given... there just isn't that much difference in the rest of it.
> (p. 248)

The results of the current study would seem to confirm this view.

CHAPTER 5

CONCLUSIONS AND IMPLICATIONS FOR PRACTICE

THIS PARTICULAR COMPARATIVE STUDY was undertaken to examine certain major theoretical assumptions about the identity challenges that adoption poses. Few empirical investigations have been concerned with the impact of one's adoptive status on the processes of identity formation during the developmental period of adolescence. Specifically, this research sought to provide needed answers to the questions of whether adoptive status adversely affects an adolescent's consolidation of ego identity, as the current literature suggests.

SUMMARY OF MAJOR FINDINGS

Contrary to theoretical expectation, when normative populations of adolescent adoptees and nonadoptees were compared along the dimension of identity formation, no significant differences emerged. Evidence suggesting that the adoptee has greater or more sustained difficulty with the tasks of adolescence was not found, indicating that adoptive status, in and of itself, is not predictive of heightened stress among adolescents in this study. In fact, the study findings seemed to suggest that, as a group, the adolescent adoptees interviewed were doing quite well.

As discussed earlier, the discrepancy between the current research findings and the bulk of adoption literature, which rather persuasively points to the intensification of identity struggles in the adolescent adoptee, may be explained on the basis of differences in sampling population. One of the unique features of this study was the use of a nonclinical population of adolescent youngsters, who, in fact, presented a less biased view of the norm.

In sharp contrast, most of the theoretical assumptions in the adoption literature have been based on clinicians' observations of adopted adolescent patients whose struggles with identity-related issues were likely to have been intensified.

An investigation of certain specific factors relating to identity outcome was undertaken next. Findings indicated that of all the variables considered, quality of family relationships was most predictive of positive identity and adjustment across all groups. Perceived openness of family communication about adoption issues was found to enhance identity formation, though it was not quite as predictive of successful outcome as the overall quality of family relationships. Finally, it was determined that family composition, as defined by the presence or absence of nonadopted siblings, had no impact whatsoever on the overall adjustment of adolescent adoptees.

Phenomenological accounts of the adoptive experience as furnished by the adoptees themselves corroborated the more quantitative findings. Adoptees as a group perceived their status rather positively, noting few ill effects emanating from adoption per se. Most, in fact, confirmed that being adopted was not that different from "natural-born status," as far as they could tell.

Some caution, however, should be taken regarding the generalizability of the present findings. All the adopted subjects in this sample were white, predominantly middle-class children placed before the age of 2 by an adoption agency (the Children's Bureau of Wilmington, Delaware), which had involved families in extensive preplacement discussion of adoption issues. In addition, maximal efforts had been made to match children with their prospective adoptive families. It is uncertain whether the results obtained would generalize to children who have been privately placed (with minimal counseling or preparation of the family), or placed later in life, although the literature certainly attests to the inherent stresses involved.

A study of search behavior in the adolescent adoptee revealed some interesting findings. Regarding the prevalence of this behavior, it was found that only a small number of subjects in this study actually expressed an interest in searching for their biological parents. Thus, in the group of 15- to 18-year-old adolescents studied, searching was not the general rule.

What differentiated adolescent searchers from those showing no proclivity in this direction? For one, searchers as a group were found to be somewhat less well adjusted than nonsearchers, although not significantly so. Furthermore, study findings indicated that searchers comprised those adolescents who perceived their family relationships to be most unsatisfactory, confirming Triseliotis's (1974) observation that unsatisfactory family ties do in fact heighten an adolescent's desire to search. It seems logical to assume that adolescents who feel most disappointed in their present relational life would be seeking to mitigate this feeling in a search for something better. Although searching seemed to have little relationship to either the style of communication about adoption issues or the presence of non-adopted siblings in the adoptive family, it was found to be more prevalent among adoptees who perceived themselves to be markedly diffcrent in appearance from their adoptive parents. Thus, mismatch issues seem to increase the likelihood of search behavior, at least as regards a perceived discrepancy in physical appearance. This seems understandable in light of the adolescent's identification needs in the process of establishing an iden-tity. The presence of role models that are too divergent might impel the adolescent adoptee toward the fantasied biological parent who offers the hope of a likeness that would allow for more comfortable identification.

Finally, with respect to the normative aspect of this study, it was found that regardless of birth status, adolescents who are most well adjusted come from families in which parental figures are able to provide a continuing source of intimacy and guidance. Thus, where parental values and influence are in balance with those of peers, identity formation proceeds comfortably along course.

IMPLICATIONS FOR PRACTICE

As mentioned at the beginning, the purpose of this research was to provide both adoptive families and practitioners with useful guidelines for positive outcome in the adopted adolescent's quest for identity. What impli-cations, then, may be drawn from the results?

The predictive strength of positive family relationships in the overall process of identity formation cannot be overemphasized. Ongoing suppor-tive educational and counseling services should be made available to adopt-ing families to facilitate the relational demands of each developmental period, especially adolescence, when the need for solid parental relation-ships is paramount. Positive identity outcome was found to occur most frequently in families that foster intimacy and attitudes of openness regard-ing issues of adoption, and where parental figures serve as influential anchors in the adolescent's relational system. Adoption services should be imple-mented with these findings in mind.

More specifically, the lack of significant differences in the adjustment of adopted and nonadopted adolescents confirms the practice of early place-ment (before the age of 2). In addition, preadoption counseling and the careful matching of children with prospective adoptive families seem to increase the likelihood of successful outcome in the adolescent years. Furth-ermore, early disclosure of adoptive status appears to have no ill effect on identity-related issues, contrary to theoretical assumptions. In fact, early dis-closure tends to be strongly advocated as good practice by most adoptees.

Agencies would do well to know that this intensely debated practice was supported by the very population for which it was designed. Finally, the presence of nonadopted siblings does not, in itself, seem to predispose the adolescent adoptee to greater stress. Again, agencies ought to be aware of this finding when making placement decisions.

It was found that search behavior lacked universality as a phenomenon in a sample of high school adolescents. On the one hand, two implications may be drawn when an interest in searching arises in this age group. Excessive genealogical concern may indicate either an impoverished relationship within the adoptive family or a felt lack of physical similarity to the adoptive parents. Adoptive parents and practitioners alike ought to be alert to the probability of these problems in the adolescent who insists on searching; excessive concern at this age might signal the need for more immediate therapeutic intervention within the adolescent's current family system.

On the other hand, adoptive parents need to be made aware that their adolescent's interest in more general information about his or her origins is a normal and healthy manifestation of the process of identity consolidation. Parents may need additional support in answering questions about their adolescent's origins—perhaps, too, an appreciation of the fact that they are, indeed, the parents with whom their adolescent identifies, regardless of the amount of questioning that occurs. Ongoing group programs of a preventive and educational nature that foster open discussion of adoption issues for adolescents and their parents are greatly needed. A prevention focus might minimize the need for therapeutic intervention.

DIRECTIONS FOR FUTURE RESEARCH

The current study represented an attempt to expand our knowledge about the impact of adoption on the adolescent years. Few normative studies in adoption have attempted to tangle with the extraordinary complexity of the adolescent experience. Because a project of this nature is as expansive and complex as the identity-related issues it seeks to study, several areas remain for consideration. Again, bear in mind that the current study findings are generalizable only to populations of white, middle-class adolescent adoptees placed as infants. Nothing has been said about the identity issues involved in racially mixed adoptions, non-infant adoptions, the physically handicapped adoptee, or adoptions of special-needs children.

Certainly, more research on normative populations of high-school-age adolescent adoptees is warranted. Further exploration and refinement of selected family variables in positive identity outcome, particularly those pertaining to aspects of family relationships, promise to yield fruitful data. Other variables that merit consideration are factors of mismatch. In the course of this research, the question arose whether extreme differences in appearance or cognitive skill of adoptees would predispose the adolescent to greater stress in the process of consolidating an identity.

The issue of search behavior in the adolescent adoptee requires more extensive investigation. Because of the limited sample of searchers in this study, any conclusions drawn must be considered tentative and subject to further refinement. Again, it would be fruitful to focus on specific dimensions of family relationships and mismatch concerns in exploring what prompts adolescents of this age to search.

In conclusion, the intricacies that adoption brings to the process of identity formation cannot be denied. Although adoptive status certainly complicates the lives of all adolescents, it is hoped that this research has served to dispel some of the dire myths that the literature has promulgated regarding the pervasiveness of identity problems in adolescent adoptees.

REFERENCES

American Academy of Pediatrics: Committee on Adoption: Identity development in adopted children. 1971, *47*, 948-949.

Austad, C. & Simmons, T.L. Symptoms of adopted children presenting to a large mental health clinic. *Child Psychiatry and Human Development,* 1978 (Fall), *9* (1), 20-27.

Barinbaum, L. Identity crisis in adolescence: The problem of an adopted girl. *Adolescence,* 1974 (Winter), *IX* (36), 547-554.

Bettelheim, B. *Children of the dream.* London: The MacMillan Company, 1969.

Blos, P. *On adolescence: A psychoanalytic interpretation.* New York: The Free Press, 1962.

Blos, P. The second individuation process of adolescence. In *Psychoanalytic study of the child.* Vol. 22, New York: International Universities Press, 1967, 162-186.

Blos, P. Character formation in adolescence. In *Psychoanalytic study of the child.* Vol. 23. New York: International Universities Press, 1968, 245-263.

Blos, P. *The young adolescent, clinical studies.* New York: The Free Press, 1970.

Blos, P. *The adolescent passage: development issues.* New York: International Universities Press, 1979.

Blum, L.H. When adoptive families ask for help. *Primary Care,* 1976 (June), *3* (2), 241-249.

Bohman, M. A study of adopted children, their background, environment and adjustment. *Acta Paediatrica Scandinavia,* 1972, *61*, 90-97.

Bourne, E. The state of research on ego identity: A review and appraisal. Part I. *Journal of Youth and Adolescence,* 1978, 7 (3), 223-251. (a)

Bourne, E. The state of research on ego identity: A review and appraisal. Part II. *Journal of Youth and Adolescence,* 1978, 7 (4), 371-392. (b)

Bowlby, J. *Attachment and loss. Vol. 1: Attachment.* New York: Basic Books, 1969.

Brodzinsky, D.M., Braff, A.M., & Singer, L.M. Adoption revelation: A cognitive-developmental perspective. Paper presented at the 10th Annual Conference on Piagetian Theory and The Helping Professions, University of Southern California, Los Angeles, January 1980.

Brodzinsky, D.M., Braff, A.M., & Singer, L.M. Children's understanding of adoption: A comparison of adopted and non-adopted children. Unpublished manuscript, Rutgers University, 1981.

Clothier, F. The psychology of the adopted child. *Mental Hygiene,* 1943, *27*, 222-230.

Coleman, J., George, R., & Holt, G. Adolescents and their parents: A study of attitudes. *Journal of Genetic Psychology,* 1977, *130*, 239-245.

Coleman, J., Herzberg, J., & Morris, M. Identity in adolescence: Present and future self-concept. *Journal of Youth and Adolescence,* 1977, 6 (1), 63-75.

Coleman, J.C. Current contradictions in adolescent theory. *Journal of Youth and Adolescence,* 1978, *7* (1), 1-11.

Constantinople, A. An Eriksonian measure of personality development. *Development Psychology,* 1969, *1,* (4), 357-372.

Dignan, M.H., Sr. Ego identity and maternal identification. *Journal of Personality and Social Psychology,* 1965, *1,* 476-483.

Douvan, E. & Adelson, J. *The adolescent experience.* New York: John Wiley & Sons, 1966.

Easson, W. Special sexual problems of the adopted adolescent. *Medical Aspects of Human Sexuality,* 1973, *17,* 92-105.

Erikson, E.H. *Childhood and society.* New York: W.W. Norton, 1950.

Erikson, E.H. The problem of ego identity. *Journal of American Psychoanalytic Association,* 1956, *4,* 56-121.

Erikson, E.H. *Identity and the life cycle—Selected papers in Psychological Issues.* Vol. 1, No. 1. New York: International Universities Press, 1959.

Erikson, E.H. (Ed.) *The challenge of youth.* New York: Basic Books, 1963 (Reprint ed. Anchor Books, 1965).

Erikson, E.H. *Identity: Youth and Crisis.* New York: W.W. Norton, 1968.

Farber, S. Sex differences in the expression of adoption ideas: Observations of adoptees from birth through latency. *American Journal of Orthopsychiatry,* 1977, *47* (4), 639-650.

Frisk, M. Identity problems and confused conceptions of the genetic ego in adopted children during adolescence. *Acta Paedo Psychiatrica,* 1964, *31,* 6-12.

Glatzer, H.T. Adoption and delinquency. *Nervous Child,* 1955, *11,* 52-56.

Goodman, J.D. & Magno-Nora, R. Adoption and its influence during adolescence. A comparison of court and community-referred psychiatric patients. *Journal of the Medical Society of New Jersey,* 1975, *72* (11), 922-928.

Goodman, J.D., Silberstein, R.M., & Mandel, W. Adopted children brought to child psychiatric clinics. *Archives of General Psychiatry,* 1963, *9,* 451-456.

Hollingshead, A.B. *The two factors index of social position.* Mimeo. New Haven, Conn., 1957.

Hoopes, J.L. *Prediction in child development: A longitudinal study of adoptive and non-adoptive families—The Delaware Family Study.* New York: Child Welfare League of America, Inc., 1982.

Hoopes, J., Sherman, E., Lawder, E., Andrews, R., & Lower, K. *A follow-up study of adoptions Post-placement functioning of adoptive children.* Vol. II. New York: Child Welfare League of America, Inc., 1970.

Josselson, R., Greenberger, E., & McConochie, D. Phenomenological aspects of psychosocial maturity in adolescence. Part I: Boys. *Journal of Youth and Adolescence,* 1977, *6* (1), 25-53. (a)

Josselson, R., Greenberger, E., & McConochie, D. Phenomenological aspects of psychosocial maturity in adolescence. Part II: Girls. *Journal of Youth and Adolescence,* 1977, *6* (2), 145-167. (b)

Kirk, H.D. *Shared fate. A theory of adoption and mental health.* New York: The Free Press, 1964.

Kirk, H.D. Jonassohn, K., & Fish, A.D. Are adopted children especially vulnerable to stress? A critique of some recent assertions. *Archives of General Psychiatry,* 1966, *14* (3), 291-298.

Lawder, E.A.; Lower, K.; Andrews, R.; Sherman, E.; and Hill, J. *A follow-up study of adoptions: Post-placement functions of adoption families.* Vol. 1. New York: Child Welfare League of America, 1969.

Lawton, J., & Gross, S. Review of the psychiatric literature on adopted children. *Archives of General Psychiatry,* 1964, *11,* 635-644.

Mahler, M.S. *On human symbiosis and the vicissitudes of individuation.* Vol. 1. New York: International Universities Press, 1968.

Mahler, M.S. On the first three subphases of the separation-individuation process. *International Journal of Psychoanalysis,* 1972, *53,* 333-338.

Mahler, M.S., Pine, F., & Bergman, A. *The psychological birth of the human infant: Symbiosis and individuation.* New York: Basic Books, 1975.

Marcia, J.E. Development and validation of ego-identity status. *Journal of Personality and Social Psychology,* 1966, *3* (5), 551-558.

Marcia, J.E. Ego identity status: Relationship to change in self-esteem, "general maladjustment" and authoritarianism. *Journal of Personality,* 1967, *35* (1), 119-133.

Marcia, J.E. Identity six years after: A follow-up study. *Journal of Youth and Adolescence,* 1976, *5,* 145-160. (a)

Marcia, J.E. *Ego identity and identity status.* Unpublished research monograph, Burnaby, British Columbia: Simon Fraser University.

Marcia, J.E. Identity in adolescence. In J. Adelson (Ed.), *Handbook of adolescent psychology.* New York: John Wiley & Sons, 1980.

McWhinnie, A.M. *Adopted children—how they grow up.* New York: Humanities Press, 1967.

McWhinnie, A.M. The adopted child in adolescence. In G. Caplan & S. Lebovici (Eds.), *Adolescence—psychosocial perspectives.* New York: Basic Books, 1969, 133-142.

Mischel, W. Direct versus indirect personality assessment: evidence and implications. *Journal of Consulting and Clinical Psychology,* 1972, *38* (3), 319-324.

Moreno, J.L. *Who shall survive? Foundations of sociometry, group psychotherapy and sociodrama.* New York: Beacon House, 1953.

Norvell, M. & Guy, Rebecca F. A comparison of self-concept in adopted and non-adopted adolescents. *Adolescence,* 1977, *12* (47), 443-448.

Nospitz, J.D. (Ed.) *Basic handbook of child psychiatry.* Vol. 1. New York: Basic Books, 1979.

Offer, D. *The psychological world of the teenager—A study of normal adolescent boys.* New York: Basic Books, 1969.

Offer, D. The Offer Self-image Questionnaire. Chicago, Ill. Dept. of Psychiatry. Michael Reese Media Center 1973.

Offer, D., Ostrov, E., & Howard, K.I. *The adolescent: A psychological self-portrait.* New York: Basic Books, 1981.

Pannor, R. & Nerlove, E. Fostering understanding between adolescents and adoptive parents through group experiences. *Child Welfare,* 1977 (Sept.-Oct.), *56* (8), 537-545.

Rickarby, G.A. & Egan, P. Issues of preventive work with adopted adolescents. *Medical Journal of Australia,* 1980 (May), *1* (10), 470-472.

Sabalis, R.F. & Burch, E.A. Comparisons of psychiatric problems of adopted and non-adopted patients. *Southern Medical Journal,* 1980, *73* (7), 867-868.

Sants, H.J. Genealogical bewilderment in children with substitute parents. *British Journal of Medical Psychology,* 1964, *37,* 133-141.

Schecter, M.D. Observations on adopted children. *Archives of General Psychiatry,* 1960, *3,* 45-56.

Schecter, M.D., Carlson, P.V., Simmons, J.Q., & Work, H.H. Emotional problems in the adoptee. *Archives of General Psychiatry,* 1964, *10,* 109-118.

Schoenberg, C. On adoption and identity. *Child Welfare,* 1974 (Nov.), *53* (9), 549.

Schwam, J.S. & Tuskan, M.K. The adopted child. In J.D. Nospitz (Ed.), *Basic Handbook of Child Psychiatry.* Vol. 1, 1979, 342-348.

Simon, N.M. & Senturia, A.G. Adoption and psychiatric illness. *American Journal of Psychiatry,* 1966, *122* (8), 858-868.

Simmons, W.V. A study of identity formation in adoptees. Dissertation Abstracts International, 1980 (June), *40* (12-B) Part I, 5832. (Order No. 8011451, University of Detroit, 1979).

Sokoloff, B. Should the adopted adolescent have access to his birth records and to his birthparents? Why? When? *Clinical Pediatrics,* 1977 (Nov.), *16* (11), 975-977.

Sorosky, A.D., Baran, A., & Pannor, R. Identity conflicts in adoptees. *American Journal of Orthopsychiatry,* 1975 (Jan.), *45* (1), 18-27.

Sorosky, A.D., Baran, A., & Pannor, R. Adoption and the adolescent: An overview. In S. C. Feinstein & P. Giovacchini (Eds.), *Adolescent psychiatry.* Vol. 5. New York: Jason Aronson Publishers, 1977, 54-72.

Spiegel, L. A. The self, the sense of self and perception. *Psychoanalytic Study of the Child,* 1959, *15,* 81-107.

Stark, P.A. & Traxler, A. J. Empirical validation of Erickson's theory of identity crisis in late adolescence. *Journal of Psychology,* 1974, 86, 25-33.

Stone, F. H. Adoption and identity. *Child Psychiatry and Human Development,* 1972 (Spring), *2* (3), 120-128.

Taichert, L. C. & Harvin, D.D. Adoption and children with learning and behavior problems. *Western Journal of Medicine,* 1975 (June), *122* (6), 464-470.

Tan, A. L., Kendis, R. F., Fine, J. T., & Porac, J. A short measure of Eriksonian Ego Identity. *Journal of Personality Assessment,* 1977, *41* (3), 279-284.

Tec, L. & Gordon, S. The adopted children's adaptation to adolescence. *American Journal of Orthopsychiatry,* 1967, *37* (2), 402.

Thomas, A., Chess, S., & Birch, H. G. *Temperament and behavior disorders in children.* New York: New York University Press, 1968.

Toussieng, P. W. Thoughts regarding the etiology of psychological difficulties in adopted children. *Child Welfare,* 1962, *41,* 59-65.

Triseliotis, J. In search of origins: the experience of adopted people. London: Routledge and Kegan Park, 1973.

Triseliotis, J. Identity and adoption. *Journal of the Association of British Adoption Agencies,* 1974, *4,* 27-34.

Wieder, H. The family romance fantasies of adopted children. *Psychoanalytic Quarterly,* 1977, *46* (2), 185-200. (a)

Wieder, H. On being told of adoption. *Psychoanalytic Quarterly,* 1977 (Jan.), *46* (1), 1-22. (b)

Wieder, H. On when and whether to disclose about adoption. *Journal of the American Psychoanalytic Association,* 1978, *26* (4), 793-811.

Witmer, H.L, Hertzog, E., Weinstein, E.A., & Sullivan, M. E. *Independent adoptions: A follow-up study.* New York: Russell Sage Foundation, 1963.

APPENDIX *A*

*S*OCIAL ATOM

*D*IRECTIONS: On a blank sheet of paper, write down the names of people (limit of 10) who are or have been most *socially* or *emotionally* significant in your life. For each person, write down the person's First Name/Age/Relationship to you and letter the names with "a," "b," "c," etc., as you go. Using a scale from 0 (lowest) to 5 (highest), place the number next to each name that best designates how *influential* that person is in your life. (*Influential* = what ability they have to change how you think and feel.) Let me know when you are finished.

Now, in front of you is another piece of paper that represents the universe. The dot in the center of the page represents *you*. Using a dot to represent each person you have already listed, place each in relation to you in your Social Atom using the following guidelines:

1. The closer you feel to the individual, place the dot closer to *you*. (Please letter your dots to correspond to the letter next to each name you designated on your first page.)
2. If the person is deceased, please use an X rather than a dot.
3. For *Adopted* Ss only: Ask after the task has been completed: Have you placed your biological parents in your Social Atom? If not, would you include them and where?

For a complete set of appendices for this volume, write to the Director of the Delaware Family Study, Dr. Janet L. Hoopes.

APPENDIX *B*

*S*EMI-STRUCTURED INTERVIEW

*P*ART I: *Questions specifically for Adopted Ss:*

1. At what age were you adopted? _____

2. How old were you when you were first told of your adoptive

   status? _____

3. At what age would you have liked to be told?
   - a. earlier ( )
   - b. same age ( )
   - c. later ( )
   - d. not at all ( )

4. Were you ever told why you were placed for adoption? Why do you

   think you were placed? _____

   _____

   _____

5. What was your reaction to being told that you were adopted?
   Very upset (1)
   Mildly distressed (2)
   Little or no negative reaction (3)

6. How sure are you that your parents told you all they know?
   Very doubtful (1)
   Unsure (2)
   Definitely convinced (3)

7. How satisfied were you with the information given to you about your adoption?
   Dissatisfied (1)
   Ambivalent (2)
   Satisfied (3)

8. Could you tell me how comfortable you think your parents feel about your adoption?
   Very comfortable/no perceved anxiety (3)
   Neutral (2)
   Uncomfortable/considerable anxiety perceived (1)

9. How openly discussed is the fact that you're adopted?
   Quite openly discussed
   Occasionally discussed
   Never mentioned.

10. When adoption is discussed *now*, how would you characterize the manner in which it is discussed? i.e., how often and how comfortably?
    a. Frequently discussed/with little to no discomfort.
    b. Frequently discussed/with marked discomfort.
    c. Occasionally discussed/with little to no discomfort
    d. Occasionally discussed/with marked discomfort.
    e. Seldom or never discussed/with little to no discomfort
    f. Seldom or never discussed/with marked discomfort.

11. How has the communication style been over the years?
    (See Question #10)

12. In your opinion, is your adoption discussed:
    Frequently enough (no change in style advocated) (3)
    With more or less appropriate frequency (2)
    With inappropriate frequency, i.e., with (1)
        not enough discussion *or*
        too much discussion

13. Some kids have wondered about their biological parents; others have
    not; even others have actually tried to obtain information about them.
    Which would you say best characterizes you?
    Actively seeking information with the intention of meeting bio-
        logical parents.
    Actively seeking information but with no intention of meeting
        biological parents.
    Wondered a lot about biological parents but never have tried to
        obtain information.
    Never wondered.

14. If you have attempted or might attempt to seek information, would
    you be interested in:
    a. Specific identifying information (name, address, telephone #,
        etc.)
    b. General information (general characteristics with no specific
        identifying information; e.g., nationality, physical characteristics,
        health, etc.)

15. Could you describe to me what you think your biological parents

    would be like? _____

    _____

    _____

    _____

    _____

    _____

16. How similar in appearance are you to your adoptive parents/family?
    Very similar physical characteristics (3)
    Somewhat similar (2)
    Strikingly different in appearance (1)

17. How do you think things would be for you if you were *not* adopted?
    a. Considerably better
    b. Slightly better
    c. No different than it is now
    d. Slightly worse
    e. Considerably more problematical

Questions for adopted and nonadopted Ss:

18. What in your estimation would be an appropriate time to tell a youngster about his/her adoption and why?
    Before 6 years
    6-12 years
    Teenage years
    Early adult years
    Never

19. Would you consider adopting a child? Why? _____

    _____

    _____

*P*ART II: *The following questions have to do with your family:*
    all Ss

20. How do you get along with your *mother* at present? How would you describe your relationship with mother?
    Compatible (3)
    Neutral (2)
    Incompatible (1)

21. How do you get along with your *father* at present? What is your relationship like with him?
    Compatible (3)
    Neutral (2)
    Incompatible (1)

22. How would you describe your relationship with your brothers and sisters at present?
    Compatible (3)
    Neutral (2)
    Incompatible (1)
    If different with specific siblings, specify: _____

    _____

    _____

23. How comfortable do you feel within your family?
    Definite sense of belonging described (3)
    Variable (2)
    Estranged (1)

24. How would you describe your role or place in the family?
    Comfortably esteemed (3)
    Neutral (2)
    Held in low regard (1)

25. How comfortable are you in having opinions that differ from those of your parents?
    Very comfortable (3)
    Somewhat comfortable (2)
    Rarely comfortable (1)

26. Have your parents been able to accept you as a separate individual with opinions of your own?
    Frequently (3)
    Occasionally (2)
    Rarely (1)

27. Are you able to disagree with your parents openly and maintain a different opinion without feeling a loss of support?
    Frequently (3)
    Occasionally (2)
    Rarely (1)

28. How able are you to negotiate differences of opinions with your mother? (Stepmother, where applicable)
    Most often able (3)
    50-50 (2)
    Rarely (1)

29. How able are you to negotiate differences of opinion with your father? (Stepfather, where applicable)
    Most often able (3)
    50-50 (2)
    Rarely (1)

30. How would you describe the way your family communicates?
    Generally smooth: communication open and easy most of the time (3)
    Occasional breakdowns in communications but generally open (2)
    Communication poor with frequent breakdowns (1)

31. What would your parents say about how you were doing in general?
    Very well (3)
    Fair (2)
    Poorly (1)

For nonadopted Ss only:

32. How do you think things would be for you if you *were* adopted?
    a. Considerably better
    b. Slightly better
    c. No different than it is now
    d. Slightly worse
    e. Considerably more problematical

For adopted Ss only:

33. Does being adopted affect how things go for you within the family?
    No effect at all (3)
    Some effect (2)
    Significant negative effect (1)

Sum   Family
       Factor

*P*ART III: *The following questions have to do with your peer group:*

34. Do you tend to have friends that you can depend on? What kinds of

    relationships are they? _____

    _____

    _____

    _____

    _____

35. How would you characterize the relationships you have?
    Warm, close, dependable relationships (3)
    Mixed (2)
    Distant or undependable relationships (1)

36. How satisfied are you with the *quality* of your friendships?
    Very satisfied (3)
    Somewhat satisfied (2)
    Dissatisfied (1)

37. How satisfied are you with the *number* of friendships you have?
    Very satisfied (3)
    Somewhat satisfied (2)
    Dissatisfied (1)

38. When you think about how other kids are doing, how would you say you are doing?
    Better than most *or* equally well (3)
    Slightly less well (2)
    Poorly (1)

39. What would other kids say about how you were doing?
    Very well (3)
    Fair (2)
    Poorly (1)

40. How open do you feel you can be with your friends about your real thoughts and feelings?
    Very open (3)
    Somewhat open (2)
    Not open at all (1)

41. Are you dating yet? How interested are you in going out with boys/girls? _____

    _____

    _____

    _____

    _____

42. How comfortable do you feel around members of the opposite sex?
    Very comfortable (3)
    Somewhat comfortable (2)
    Uncomfortable (1)

43. How attractive do you feel you are to members of the opposite sex?
    Attractive (3)
    Average (2)
    Unattractive (1)

For adopted Ss only:

44. How open do you feel you can be with your friends about your adoption?
    Very open (3)
    Selectively open (2)
    Closed (1)

45. What kind of effect does being adopted have upon your feelings of acceptance by peers?
    No effect at all (3)
    Some effect (2)
    Significantly negative effect (1)

46. What kind of effect has your adoption had upon your ability to date or feel comfortable with opposite sex peers?
    No effect at all (3)
    Some effect (2)
    Significant negative effect (1)

Sum   Peer
      Factor

*P*ART IV: *The following questions have to do with school:*

47. How would you say you are doing in school? That is, what kind of a student would you say you are?
    Above average (3)
    Average (2)
    Below average (1)

48. What would your teachers say about how you are doing?
    Above average (3)
    Average (2)
    Below average (1)

49. What would your parents say about how you were doing in school?
    Very well (3)
    Fair (2)
    Poorly (1)

50. Does your performance in your subjects provide you with any good feelings?
    Rarely/never (1)
    Occasionally (2)
    Frequently (3)

For adopted Ss only:

51. Do your teachers know that you are adopted? _____

_____

_____

52. If so, (see #51) does this knowledge have any effect upon their interaction with you?
    No effect at all (3)
    Some effect (2)
    Significant negative effect (1)

53. What kind of effect does being adopted have upon your academic functioning?
    Significant negative effect (1)
    Some effect (2)
    No effect at all (3)

Sum   School   [ ]
       Factor

PART V: *The following questions relate to your feelings about yourself:*

54. How comfortable do you generally feel with yourself?
    Comfortable most of the time (3)
    Comfortable some of the time (2)
    Rarely comfortable (1)

55. Relative to others, how attractive do you feel physically?
    Quite attractive (3)
    Somewhat attractive (2)
    Not attractive at all (1)

56. Relative to others, how attractive a personality do you think you have?
    Quite attractive (3)
    Somewhat attractive (2)
    Not attractive at all (1)

57. What types of characteristics, in your opinion, make you seem

    attractive to others? _____

    _____

    _____

    _____

    _____

58. If you changed some aspects of yourself for the better, how much change would there have to be?
    Considerable change (1)
    Some change (2)
    Little change (3)

59. What kind of change would you desire? _____

_____

_____

_____

_____

60. How close are you to becoming that person you most want to be?
    Very close (3)
    Moderately close (2)
    Far away (1)

61. What kind of opinion do you hold of yourself?
    Poor opinion (1)
    So-so opinion of yourself (2)
    Good opinion of yourself (3)

For adopted Ss only:

62. Has being adopted had any effect upon your opinion of yourself?
    No effect at all (3)
    Some effect (2)
    Considerable negative effect (1)

Sum   Self-Esteem
       Factor